CONTENTS

THE WEDDING
OF THE CENTURY

On Friday 29 April 2011, millions of people in the United Kingdom were given the day off. Children did not have to go to school and many businesses around the country were closed because it was a bank holiday.

WHAT IS A BANK HOLIDAY?

In the United Kingdom, a bank holiday is a national public holiday. They are called "bank" holidays because banks and the stock market are closed and are not able to do business. These public holidays are set in law or announced by royal proclamation each year. England and Wales each have eight bank holidays a year, including New Year's Day,

Good Friday and Boxing Day. Scotland has nine bank holidays including St Andrew's Day, and Northern Ireland has ten including St Patrick's Day.

In the United Kingdom, extra bank holidays can be added by royal proclamation to allow people to mark important national occasions such as the wedding or funeral of a senior member of the royal family or to celebrate a monarch's jubilee.

But 29 April was no ordinary bank holiday. This one was given to the British public to celebrate what promised to be the wedding of the century.

For weeks before the big day, reporters speculated over which designer the bride might have chosen to create her dress, which tiara she would select, what kind of wedding cake the couple would have and who, out of their many celebrity friends, they would invite to the service

Richmond upon Thames Libraries

Renew online at www.richmond.gov.uk/libraries

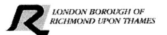
LONDON BOROUGH OF
RICHMOND UPON THAMES

WILLIAM & CATHERINE

A LIFE STORY

Sally Morgan

Illustrated by **Mike Phillips**

SCHOLASTIC

Published in the UK by Scholastic, 2023
1 London Bridge, London, SE1 9BG
Scholastic Ireland, 89E Lagan Road, Dublin Industrial Estate, Glasnevin,
Dublin, D11 HP5F

SCHOLASTIC and associated logos are trademarks and/or
registered trademarks of Scholastic Inc.

Text © Sally Morgan, 2023
Cover illustration by Sarah Papworth © Scholastic, 2023
Inside illustrations by Mike Phillips in the style of Sarah Papworth
© Scholastic, 2023

ISBN 978 07023 2862 6

A CIP catalogue record for this book is available from the British Library.

Printed by CPI Group (UK) Ltd, Croydon, CR0 4YY
Paper made from wood grown in sustainable forests and other controlled
sources.

1 3 5 7 9 10 8 6 4 2

www.scholastic.co.uk

and to entertain guests at their reception.

But why was everyone so excited? Couples get married every day, and while their friends and close families may choose to take time off work, the rest of the country goes about their day as normal. In fact, unless something very remarkable takes place, such as the ceremony being delayed by a swarm of angry bees (this has actually happened), or a celebrity guest appearing at the reception, 99.9 per cent of weddings are very unlikely to make the news, never mind every television bulletin and the front page of every national newspaper.

The excitement was because this was no ordinary wedding – it was the wedding of the future king, Prince William.

Prince William – Grandson and Heir

Prince William is the grandson of the late Queen Elizabeth II, and the eldest son of King Charles III (formerly the Prince of Wales) and his first wife Diana, Princess of Wales. As the eldest son of the current monarch, Prince William will become king when King Charles III dies.

Prince William is a member of the British royal family, which has been known as the House of Windsor since 1917 when King George V replaced the family name Saxe-Coburg-Gotha. He made the change during the First World War because the name sounded too German, whereas Windsor sounded more patriotic.

A MODERN(ISH) MONARCHY

In the United Kingdom we have a monarchy. Countries with a monarchy have a king, queen, emperor or empress as their head of state.

The United Kingdom is known as a "constitutional monarchy". This means that the king or queen is the head of the state – that is, of the nation – but they do not get to do whatever they want. They don't get to make laws and are expected to abide by a set of rules known as the constitution. In the United Kingdom, new laws and amendments to the constitution are proposed by the government, which is led by the prime minister and agreed by parliament.

Unlike the prime minister, who in the UK is chosen by the party that has been elected to govern the country, a monarch inherits their position from a relative, usually their mother or father.

King Charles III became king on 8 September 2022 on the death of his mother Elizabeth II, who in turn became queen on 6 February 1952 when her father, King George VI, died.

The royal wedding was a cause for national celebration. People from all over the country travelled to London up to three days before the ceremony to secure a prime position near Buckingham Palace or the church selected for the wedding – Westminster Abbey.

WESTMINSTER ABBEY

Westminster Abbey is a church in central London near the Houses of Parliament. There has been a church on the site for more than a thousand years. The wedding of William and Catherine was the latest in a long line of royal events held at the abbey. All English monarchs who have had a coronation since William the Conqueror in 1066 have been crowned at Westminster Abbey and it is the final resting place of thirty kings and queens. The original building was completed by Edward the Confessor in 1065. Much of the current abbey dates back to 1245 and the reign of King Henry III.

As well as weddings and coronations, Westminster Abbey has been the setting for funerals, including that of Prince William's mother, Princess Diana, in 1997, and Queen Elizabeth II in 2022.

Shops stocked up on specially made items to celebrate the occasion, selling everything from blankets to biscuit tins, all printed with smiling portraits of the prince and his long-time girlfriend, fiancée and soon-to-be wife, Kate Middleton.

Catherine "Kate" Elizabeth Middleton

Catherine Middleton was born in Berkshire in 1982. Catherine is the daughter of Michael and Carole Middleton. Catherine's mother and father both worked for British Airways before starting a business selling party supplies.

William and Catherine had known each other for many years, meeting in their first year at university. They became a couple in their second year of university and lived with one another.

The Commoner's Touch

William and Catherine's wedding was a historic occasion, not only because it was the wedding of the future king, but because of who he was marrying. Catherine Middleton was not from a noble family, which meant that neither her mother, father nor any of her relatives had a title, such as duke or duchess, lord or lady. She, like 99 per cent of people living in the United Kingdom, was what is known as a "commoner".

Traditionally, members of the royal family, particularly heirs to the throne, were not allowed to marry commoners, but were instead expected to marry high-ranking distant relatives, or members of foreign royal families. Prince William is related to most of the monarchs in Europe.

William's father, Charles, had chosen his first wife from a noble family. Princess Diana, formerly Lady Diana Spencer, was the daughter of an earl and a member of the Spencer family, who were good friends with the royal family and had been for generations. Diana's grandmothers had been ladies-in-waiting (a formal type of close friend) to Prince William's great grandmother, the Queen Mother.

A Gift from Granny

But Catherine wouldn't be a commoner for much longer. It is a tradition that the monarch gives senior members of the royal family and their spouses titles when they marry, as a wedding gift and a symbol of their new role as a married couple. Prince William was no different. He and Catherine were given the titles of the Duke and Duchess of Cambridge in England and Wales, Baron and Baroness Carrickfergus in Northern Ireland and the Earl and Countess of Strathearn in Scotland.

Members of the royal family have different titles in Scotland as it was a separate country until 1701, when it joined England and Wales to form the United Kingdom.

A Family Affair

Inside the abbey, William stood in his military uniform and waited by the high altar. His brother Prince Harry stood alongside him. When Catherine entered the abbey, William smiled as the Choirs of Westminster and Her Majesty's Chapel Royal, St James's Palace, sang out. Wearing a lace and ivory-satin gown, Catherine was accompanied by her father, Michael, and carried a bouquet of myrtle, lily of the valley, sweet william and hyacinths. Catherine walked slowly up the aisle, which had been transformed into an avenue of field maple and hornbeam trees – a symbol of the couple's love of the countryside. As Catherine walked, she passed guests including celebrities such as David Beckham and Sir Elton John and politicians such as Prime Minister David Cameron. As she neared the altar, she passed William's father, Charles, Prince of Wales, seated next to his wife, Camilla, Duchess of Cornwall, and William's grandmother, Her Majesty Queen Elizabeth II herself.

"You look lovely. You look beautiful," William said as he greeted his bride. Then he turned to her father and joked, "We were supposed to have just a small family affair."

First Steps into the Future

As William and his bride left the abbey, crowds of people cheered for the happy couple and wished them well. As a member of one of the most famous families in the world, the people in the crowd had watched William as he grew up and they felt that they knew him. Some had watched his father, Prince Charles, grow up too, and some even remembered his grandmother coming to the throne. But William's new bride was another story. Who was this new duchess and future queen? Where had she come from, and what would she and William do next? And what would this new royal couple mean for the future of the monarchy?

A COLD RECEPTION

The warmth of the crowd that greeted Catherine as she left Westminster Abbey was a stark contrast to the freezing temperatures that welcomed her when she was born on 9 January 1982. That January was one of the coldest on record. Thick snow and ice covered the roads as Carole Middleton, pregnant with her first baby, went into labour. Her husband Michael was on his way home to drive her to hospital, but he worked as a flight dispatcher at London's Heathrow Airport, which was more than forty-five minutes' drive away. Carole waited at home, worried she wouldn't make it to the hospital in time for her baby to be born.

Carole called her doctor to say she thought her baby was on the way and that she was worried about getting to the hospital in time. Her doctor reassured her that first babies often took their time, but if her baby proved to be an exception, he would send an air ambulance to get her.

But Michael did make it home and he did get Carole to the Royal Berkshire Hospital in time for her to give birth to their little girl. Michael and Carole named their baby girl Catherine Elizabeth, but called her Kate.

Meet the Parents

Before Carole had Catherine, she was a flight attendant for British Airways. For Carole, her job was a dream come true.

Carole's family didn't have much money while

she was growing up. She wanted to be a teacher, but while she did well at school, her parents couldn't afford to send her to university. Instead Carole left school at the age of sixteen and started work in a clothes shop. It was fun, but Carole was ambitious and wanted more. In 1974, she applied to become a flight attendant. Her family, like most families in England at the time, hadn't travelled outside of England much, so Carole saw working for an airline as an opportunity to see the world. In the 1970s, flying was much more of a luxury than it is today. Flight attendants were well paid and considered very glamorous. The training was hard and there were strict rules about how you looked, such as the nail varnish you could wear and how long your hair should be. However, applicants who passed the training could look forward to a rewarding job.

Carole met her husband Michael at work. As a flight dispatcher, Michael managed the British Airways flights in and out of the airport. He also organized the schedules for restocking food and refuelling the aircraft between flights.

Michael Middleton came from a wealthier background than Carole. His grandparents had even hosted members of the royal family at their home in the 1920s, and they had left him a trust fund, a sum of money that his parents used to send him to private school and university. While he was growing up, Michael dreamed of becoming a pilot. His father, Captain Peter Middleton, had flown with the Royal Air Force (RAF) during the Second World War. In 1962, Peter was co-pilot to Prince Philip on a tour of South America, and

Michael was inspired by his father's exciting stories about flying. After university, Michael trained as a pilot at the British European Airways Flight School, but soon realized that life in the cockpit wasn't for him. Instead, he trained as a member of the ground crew and became a flight dispatcher.

Michael and Carole married on 21 June 1980 at a small church in the village of Dorney in Buckinghamshire. The reception was held at Dorney Court, a manor house near Windsor, and while it seemed a fancy affair for members of Carole's family, it was a far cry from the reception of a royal wedding.

A Cottage on Cock Lane

Michael and Carole's first home was a red-brick cottage in a village named Bradfield Southend in Berkshire. When Carole discovered she was pregnant in 1981 she left her job and concentrated on transforming their little house on Cock Lane into the perfect home for their baby.

Carole and Michael were excited to become

new parents. While they didn't have a lot of money, they were determined that their little girl would be treated like a princess. They bought the best pram they could afford and threw a big party to celebrate her christening on 20 June 1982. Even though she was a busy new mother, Carole made all the cakes and sandwiches herself, and Michael made sure there was lots of champagne.

WHAT IS A CHRISTENING?

A christening is a religious ceremony in which a person is welcomed into the Christian faith. During the service, a minister sprinkles or pours water on the head of the person being christened. The water used in the ceremony is known as holy water and has been blessed by a church official known as a clergyman.

Mummy and Me

Carole attended mother-and-baby groups with Catherine, where she made friends with other mothers from the village. Carole enjoyed being part of village life and being a mother. She would load Kate into her pram and take long walks in the countryside with her new friends.

On 6 September 1983, Carole and Michael welcomed another little girl into their lives – Philippa Charlotte Middleton, known to everyone as Pippa. To give Carole time to spend with the new baby, Catherine started attending a playgroup in the village's church hall.

With two children, Carole and Michael were happy, but they were too adventurous to live their whole lives in a rural village. It was cosy and comfortable, but the Middletons wanted to see more of the world. In 1984, they got that chance.

A Duchess in the Desert

Working for an airline meant that Michael was sometimes given the opportunity to live and work in other countries. In 1984, when he was asked if he would like to work at a new airport in Amman, Jordan, Carole and Michael jumped at the chance. Amman was a hot and bustling city, as different from Bradfield Southend as they could imagine.

THE HASHEMITE KINGDOM OF JORDAN

Amman is the capital of the Hashemite Kingdom of Jordan. Jordan is a country in the Middle East, which borders Saudi Arabia, Syria, Israel, the Palestinian territory of the West Bank, and Iraq. The fertile valley of the River Jordan runs through the country, but the rest of Jordan consists of arid mountains and desert where temperatures can reach 40°C. People have lived in Jordan for hundreds of thousands of years and many of them, including the Babylonians and Romans, left behind ancient buildings and monuments.

Today the majority of people living in Jordan are Muslim, practising Islam. The national language is Arabic. Like the United Kingdom, Jordan has a constitutional monarchy, though the Jordanian constitution allows the king more control over the government than the UK's leader has. In 1984, the king of Jordan was King Hussein, who came to the throne in 1952, the same year as Queen Elizabeth II. Following his death in 1999, King Hussein was succeeded by his son, King Abdullah II.

Carole and Michael found a house with a flat roof in a quiet neighbourhood. The house had a garden with a swing for Catherine. She had her own room in which she showed her early flair for interior design, decorating the walls and furniture with Mickey Mouse stickers. British Airways paid their rent and for a car for Michael to travel to and from work. They also gave the Middletons free flights home, so they could visit their family often.

Just as in the village, Carole soon became a part of the local community and enrolled Catherine in the nursery near their home.

An International Early-Years Education

The nursery taught children in both English and Arabic. Catherine and her fellow students learned to sing nursery rhymes and to count in both languages. They also learned stories from the Qur'an, the holy book of Islam.

At nursery Kate enjoyed playing in the sandpit and experimenting with the dressing-up box. The nursery also had a playhouse where Kate would invite her classmates to tea parties. She went on field trips to the zoo and to the market in the city. The pupils had to hold on to a beaded line to make sure they didn't wander off and get lost.

Carole dropped Catherine off at nursery in the morning before going home and looking after Pippa, often taking her on walks with mothers living nearby. Michael picked Catherine up when he finished work in the afternoon. In the evenings Michael and Carole invited their friends over for parties. At the weekend, when Michael wasn't working, they would explore Jordan's historic sites such as Petra and Jerash.

Bon Voyage

After two and a half years in Amman, the Middletons decided it was time to return home. So in 1986, Michael and Carole said goodbye to their friends, packed up their home and took their children back to the cottage on Cock Lane. Although they enjoyed the warm weather in

Jordan, and being able to spend so much time outdoors, it was always their plan to return home in time for Catherine to start school, and that time was approaching fast.

THE LITTLE PRINCE

The birth of the Middletons' babies was a cause for celebration for Carole and Michael's immediate family, and for the local community. But around the time of Catherine's christening, people all over the country and around the world waited for news of the birth of a baby to one of the planet's most famous couples. A couple who, little under a year ago, had captured the imagination of millions when they married at St Paul's Cathedral, London.

THE WEDDING OF CHARLES, PRINCE OF WALES, AND LADY DIANA SPENCER

On 29 July 1981, Prince Charles, eldest son of Queen Elizabeth II and first in line to the throne of the United Kingdom, married Lady

Diana Spencer at a ceremony at St Paul's Cathedral, London.

The wedding was straight out of the pages of a fairy tale. Diana, then just twenty years old, travelled to the cathedral in a horse-drawn glass coach complete with liveried footmen. When Diana arrived, she stepped out to reveal a billowing ivory-silk gown with a train that was more than seven metres long. After the ceremony, the couple travelled to Buckingham Palace in an open-topped carriage and waved to some of the 600,000 people who had come to London to celebrate their special day. At the palace, the newlyweds stepped out onto the balcony with their family and kissed, much to the delight of the cheering crowd. A record-breaking audience of 750 million in seventy-four countries watched the wedding on television.

On 21 June 1982, just before 10 p.m., Buckingham Palace posted an announcement on an easel outside the gates.

"Her Royal Highness the Princess of Wales was safely delivered of a son at 9.03 p.m. today. Her Royal Highness and her child are both doing well."

On the steps of St Mary's Hospital, London, a very tired but delighted Prince Charles greeted the press who had been waiting outside for hours. The prince confirmed that his wife was doing well, but that they were struggling to agree on a name for their little prince.

"WE HAVE THOUGHT OF ONE OR TWO NAMES, THERE'S A BIT OF AN ARGUMENT OVER IT."

King Charles III, then Prince of Wales

The fountains of Trafalgar Square and other buildings around London were lit up in blue and people gathered in the street to celebrate the birth of the new baby, chanting and singing, "It's a boy, it's a boy, it's a boy," and, "Well done Charlie, let's have another one."

News of the baby's birth spread fast and caused an avalanche of good wishes from all over the world. On the lawn of the White House in the United States, President Ronald Reagan, who had been meeting with British Prime Minister Margaret Thatcher, asked her to forward his congratulations to the prince and princess.

"WE HAVE EVERY HOPE THAT SHE WILL CARRY BACK TO LONDON OUR FONDEST GOOD WISHES, THOSE OF THE AMERICAN PEOPLE, NANCY AND MYSELF, TO THEIR ROYAL HIGHNESSES THE PRINCE AND PRINCESS OF WALES, AND TO THEIR LITTLE SON."

President Ronald Reagan

President Reagan later sent the new parents an antique child-sized chair with an embroidered seat cushion. All around the United Kingdom, school children made cards to congratulate the Prince and Princess of Wales on the new baby. Many thousands of gifts and cards were sent to the new baby and his parents, but they didn't get to keep most of them. Gifts from foreign leaders were kept in the royal collection, but other presents such as flowers, baby clothes and food were donated to members of staff or to nearby hospitals.

What's in a Name?

The reporters were vying with one another to get the scoop on what the royal couple were going to name the new baby. The public were interested too, some even placing bets on the name they thought most likely. George was the favourite, after Charles's grandfather and great grandfather, King George VI and King George V, followed by James and then Charles. But if you had put money on any of those names, you would have come away empty-handed when the palace announced on 28 June that the new prince was named William Arthur Philip Louis.

The Royal Apartments

Baby William's first home was an apartment in Kensington Palace. The apartment was given to the Prince and Princess of Wales by the queen as a London home to start their family. It had twenty-four rooms, which included bedrooms, living rooms and offices. It also had a yellow and white nursery, which Charles and Diana had decorated with illustrations from Beatrix Potter. Rather than a single room, the nursery was actually a whole suite of rooms, which included a bedroom for William, a dining room and a sitting room, as well as a playroom. There were also rooms for William's nannies, Barbara Barnes and Olga Powell.

Kensington Palace

Prince Charles had described his own childhood as being rather lonely, but William's was far from that. Kensington Palace wasn't a single home but a collection of apartments filled with relatives, including five cousins under the age of eight. Charles referred to Kensington Palace as "the aunt heap". These aunts included his own aunt and the queen's sister, Princess Margaret, and William's aunt and his mother's sister, Jane Fellowes, whose husband worked for the royal family.

At weekends, William, his mother and father and the nannies all travelled to Highgrove, which was Charles's house in the country. Highgrove was a large house surrounded by gardens designed by Prince Charles, and a farm. Charles was excited to become a father and looked forward to spending time in the outdoors with his son.

HIGHGROVE HOUSE

In 1980, Charles bought a home in Gloucestershire called Highgrove House. The house had nine bedrooms and an enormous garden. Both the inside and the outside needed a lot of work, but Charles wanted to make the place his own, for himself and his future family. After he married, Diana helped him redesign the house. He was more interested in the grounds, where he created a cottage garden, a meadow of wildflowers and an arboretum.

There was also a swimming pool, a climbing frame and a farm teeming with animals, including a duck pond. Charles loved being outdoors and hoped his children would learn to love it too. He also built a tree house, which he named "Holyrood House" after the royal palace in Edinburgh.

As well as Kensington Palace and Highgrove, William travelled between the royal family's other residences, such as Windsor Castle, Sandringham in Norfolk, and Balmoral and Birkhall in Scotland.

A Royal Christening

On 4 August 1982, Prince William Arthur Philip Louis was christened in the white and gold music room of Buckingham Palace.

Prince William was dressed in the same ivory-silk christening gown his father had worn nearly thirty-four years before, as had previous generations of royal babies.

THE SECOND-HAND GOWN

The christening gown worn by the prince was known as the Honiton Lace Gown and was made for Princess Victoria, the eldest daughter of Queen Victoria. The gown was then used for every royal christening, until a replica gown was commissioned by Queen Elizabeth II in 2004. The replica gown has been used for the christenings of Prince George, Princess Charlotte and Prince Louis, and Prince Harry's son Archie.

After the ceremony the family posed for photographs, including one extra-special picture of William in the arms of his great grandmother the Queen Mother, who was celebrating her eighty-second birthday on the same day.

QUEEN ELIZABETH – THE QUEEN MOTHER

Queen Elizabeth, the Queen Mother, was the mother of Queen Elizabeth II, and widow of King George VI. Elizabeth Angela Marguerite Bowes-Lyon was born in London and grew up at Glamis Castle in Scotland. Glamis Castle is famous for being one of the most haunted homes in the United Kingdom and is the setting of *Macbeth*, the play by William Shakespeare. Elizabeth married Prince Albert, Duke of York, in 1923, and had two daughters. When Albert's elder brother, King Edward VIII, abdicated (stepped down from) the throne, Albert became the new king and Elizabeth was his queen. When a person becomes the monarch, they are allowed to choose a new name. Albert chose the name George after his father, and became King George VI.

After the photographs, William was fed and given to his nanny and the family gathered for lunch to celebrate the Queen Mother's birthday.

The christening was a difficult day for Diana. The ceremony was scheduled at the time William usually ate, so he was grumpy. With no sense of the importance of the occasion, the young prince was restless and hungry, and cried loudly. Diana felt under pressure to calm him down, which was difficult with so many people around. Diana was overwhelmed, which was a feeling she'd had a lot since William was born because she was suffering from a condition called postnatal depression, which can make it very difficult to cope in the first months of parenthood.

The Prince Down Under

Both Charles and Diana loved William very much and enjoyed spending time with him. Diana in particular didn't like being separated from him, but as members of the royal family, they both had royal duties they were expected to fulfil. These duties included visiting countries where Queen Elizabeth II was head of state, on royal tours. When Charles was little, his mother had often travelled on royal tours and left him at home with his grandmother and his nannies. Diana didn't want to leave William behind, so when he was just nine months old, the royal couple took him and his nannies on his first royal tour – to Australia and New Zealand.

WHAT IS A ROYAL TOUR?

A royal tour is when members of the royal family travel overseas to visit countries where the monarch of the United Kingdom is head of state. These countries are known as Commonwealth Realms.

In 2023, King Charles III is head of state in fifteen Commonwealth Realms, including Australia, New Zealand, Canada, Grenada, Jamaica, Antigua and Barbuda, Belize, the Bahamas, Papua New Guinea, Saint Kitts and Nevis, Saint Lucia, Saint Vincent and the Grenadines, the Solomon Islands, Tuvalu and the United Kingdom.

When on tour, working royals act as ambassadors for the United Kingdom. They visit schools and charities, and they meet with leaders and local officials, as well as lots of well-wishers who turn up for a chance to catch a glimpse of a real king, queen, prince or princess.

The tour was hard work. Every minute of Charles and Diana's day was filled with visits and walkabouts. William's parents were two of the most recognizable people in the world, so everywhere they went they were greeted by crowds of people, cheering and wanting to shake their hands. Diana was a particular favourite. She was young, stylish and hugely popular. Photographers vied with one another to get the best shot of her and these pictures appeared in the newspapers almost every day. As Charles and Diana toured the country, William stayed with his nannies at place called Woomargama Station in New South Wales.

Even though he was only nine months old, William was a natural star with a big personality. At a photo call with the world's press, he showed off his new crawling skills on a blanket as his parents sat on either side of him.

As well as commenting on Diana's style and her way with people, journalists wrote about what a loving mother she was.

Diana got a lot of attention back home too. Independent photographers, known as paparazzi, tried to follow her wherever she went. The paparazzi sold the pictures they took to whichever newspaper offered them the most money. Photographs of Diana sold for many thousands of pounds so the paparazzi went to great lengths to get them, such as using cameras with powerful lenses. One photographer even managed to photograph Diana through the windows at Highgrove.

Missed Milestone

Diana and Charles didn't take William with them on their next official visit – an eighteen-day tour of Canada. They thought the short trip would be too disruptive for the young prince and worried that spending time on the royal yacht in rough seas would be too much for him. The tour meant they would be away for William's first birthday.

Diana called William's nannies twice a day. She tried to speak to William too, but he was too little to talk for long on the phone. The tour, which included visits to Nova Scotia, Prince Edward Island and Ottawa, finished in

Edmonton, where more than seventy thousand people showed up to see them, though Diana was the main attraction.

"We want Di! We want Di! We want Di!" shouted the crowd.

While in Edmonton, Diana celebrated her twenty-second birthday. She was treated to a rendition of "Happy Birthday" sung by an entire stadium of people. Charles was jealous of the attention Diana was getting, but Diana found the constant hubbub a strain.

William Turns One

With his parents away, William celebrated his birthday with his nannies, Barbara and Olga, then had a proper party when his parents returned home. The party was a private event, but that didn't stop the press speculating as to who would be at what they called the "year's most exclusive party", which they said would be celebrated with his cousins, Charles and Diana's godchildren. It wouldn't be long before William had a sibling to play with.

A Playmate for a Prince

On 16 September 1984, Prince Charles took William to St Mary's Hospital in London to see his mother and to meet his baby brother born the previous day – Prince Henry Charles Albert David, who soon became known to everyone as Harry.

His Royal Naughtiness

With a new baby in the home, the Prince and Princess of Wales had their hands full and were glad of the help of their nannies. William's favourite nanny was named Barbara Barnes, but William called her Baba.

William was a boisterous child. From the moment he could walk, he didn't stop. Diana referred to him as a "holy terror" because he caused destruction wherever he went. His other nickname was "Basher Wills".

Both Charles and Diana were gentle, loving parents to their boys and tried never to yell at them, even when they were naughty. They also forbade their nannies from shouting at them and they were certainly never allowed to smack them, even though that was not an uncommon form of punishment for children at the time.

The Prince Goes to Nursery

In 1956, William's father became the first heir to the British throne to go to school when he attended Hill House in West London. Before that, he was educated by a private tutor at Buckingham Palace. Thirty years later in September 1985, when William was just over three years old, he achieved his own first when he became the first heir to the throne to go to nursery. Charles and Diana chose a nursery called Miss Mynors' in Notting Hill, London, a short distance from Kensington Palace. Diana wanted William to be treated the same as other children and to have the same experiences. But William's life was often very different to that of his friends. They attended the same nursery, but the other pre-schoolers weren't greeted on their first day by a pack of reporters and photographers, calling to them to look over so they could get the perfect picture.

Thankfully this didn't happen every day. The palace made a deal with the reporters to allow them to publish pictures taken on his first day if they left him and the students' families alone afterwards. This was to ensure that William and the other children could learn in peace.

William loved being at nursery. Harry was still too little to be much fun, so he enjoyed being able to play with other children his own age. While he may have been a terror at home, he was popular at school and made friends easily.

But getting him to school wasn't so easy. William was stubborn and would not be told what to do. He insisted on choosing his own clothes and neither Diana nor Charles wanted to argue, so he often wore what he wanted even if it wasn't suitable. Sometimes William regretted his choices, and his parents hoped he would learn from his mistakes. He soon did. On a chilly weekend at Highgrove, William had refused to put on his gloves. Once he was outside, his hands were so cold that he started to cry. Charles did not have much sympathy for his son and told him to be quiet because it was his own fault.

As well as learning all the usual things at pre-school, such as his letters and numbers, outside school William learned to ride.

William had been around horses since he was very little. The queen loved horses and had passed this love on to Charles, who was keen for his son to learn to ride. When William was four he started taking lessons. William's first mount was a Shetland pony called Smokey that was kept at his father's stables at Highgrove, but would be transported to Balmoral and Sandringham whenever William was staying there. William soon became a good rider and was sometimes even allowed to lead his two-year-old brother Harry around on Smokey, holding the pony's lead tight.

Bye Bye Baba

William's mother worried he was growing too close to his Nanny Baba. Diana had a busy schedule and couldn't be at home as often as she would like, so she and Charles relied on William's nannies. But Diana didn't like that William ran to Nanny Baba when he was hurt, and that Baba was the first person he asked for when he woke up. Diana felt William should ask for her instead.

One day when William got home from nursery, he had a nasty surprise – his beloved Baba was gone. This made William upset and confused and he worried that he might have been too naughty and driven her away. But instead, while he was at nursery, his mother had asked the nanny to leave and didn't even give her the chance to say goodbye. William had another nanny, but he missed Baba and wondered if she would ever come back.

William Goes to Work

On 23 July 1986, William was a pageboy at his uncle Prince Andrew's wedding, which was his first official public engagement. Instead of doing what he was told, William pulled faces and fidgeted, and stuck out his tongue, all of which was noticed, not only by the press but also by his grandmother the queen. After the ceremony, the queen told Diana and Charles that even though

William was little, she expected more from a boy who would one day be king and said that he needed more discipline.

But William's behaviour wasn't the biggest problem in Charles and Diana's household. Since their wedding, Charles and Diana found that rather than growing closer, they had grown further apart. She was particularly resentful about a friend he had known for many years, an ex-girlfriend named Camilla Parker Bowles. Charles didn't understand Diana's dramatic mood swings, and did not sympathize with her struggles with her mental health. When they were together or spoke on the phone, Charles and Diana argued a lot, and as time passed they found it easier to live separate lives.

But the couple had to be together sometimes for public engagements. While there were rumours in the press that Charles and Diana were unhappy in their marriage, they did their best to look united when they appeared in public.

They also had to get together to make decisions about where to send William to school. They didn't agree on many things, but both wanted William and Harry to have happier childhoods than their own, as well the best possible education. The couple kept all of this in mind when making their decision on William's next step.

FAR FROM THE PALACE

Meanwhile, the Middletons were preparing for Catherine's next steps too. The move home from Amman was a big adjustment for Catherine. While she had lived in Berkshire for the first two years of her life, Amman was the only home she remembered. It was where she made friends at nursery. It was where her hair went blonde in the sun while playing in the garden on her swing and in her paddling pool. Catherine had attended nursery in Amman and her parents taught her at home too. Michael and Carole raised their children to have good manners and be polite. They treated their children with respect and expected them to show the same courtesy to others.

School Time

Shortly after Catherine turned four, her parents enrolled her in a local private school. Private schools are not funded by the government – they raise money by charging fees. These schools don't have to follow the national curriculum and they can cost a pupil's family many thousands of pounds a year.

Before they had left for Amman, Michael and Carole met with the headmaster of St Andrew's, a private fee-paying school near their home. The Middletons told the headmaster that they had heard good things about the school and wanted Catherine to attend when they returned home. Even though they were not wealthy, there was still enough in Michael's trust fund for him to send his children to St Andrew's.

Catherine was looking forward to starting school, but first she had to get kitted out. St Andrew's required pupils to wear a school uniform. Catherine's uniform was a blue-green blazer worn over a white blouse and a blue skirt. She also had to wear a black tie. If it was cold, pupils could put on green sweaters. It was a lot of clothes for a girl used to wearing shorts and T-shirts!

Catherine adjusted to her uniform and her new school quickly. She was full of energy and interested in sports, and became known for tearing about the school and climbing trees in the grounds. Catherine's teachers described her as enthusiastic, happy and a delight to teach. She worked hard in the classroom and pushed herself at games, winning medals at the school sports days.

Party Time

While Catherine was at school, Carole took her sister Pippa to the playgroup in the church hall and got reacquainted with the other mums living in the village. While Carole was talking to them, she discovered that many of them struggled to find fun items for their children's birthday parties. Carole loved throwing parties for her children. She loved entertaining and believed that birthdays were an extra-special occasion.

Carole wanted to find out more, so she asked questions – lots of them. She asked people what they wanted for their children's parties and what they struggled to find, and she also asked how much they were willing to pay. Carole wasn't being nosy asking these questions, she was doing something called "market research", to find out whether she could make a business out of supplying people with novelties for their children's parties. After completing her research, Carole believed that she could.

Carole started small, putting together party bags and selling them in the local church hall. The bags contained sweets and small gifts, and were the perfect tokens to send home with kids after a party. Carole's party bags sold quickly. Busy parents were happy that the work of putting together the gifts was done for them and were happy to pay for it. News of Carole's party bags spread, and soon Carole was selling them elsewhere.

Carole put the party bags together at her kitchen table. She was busy with her two children and her new business when she found out she was going to have another baby.

And Then There Were Three

On 15 April 1987, the Middletons welcomed a son, James William, into their home. Catherine and Pippa were very happy to have a little brother. They loved to help their mother and father look after him, giving him baths and keeping him entertained.

It was a busy time for the family. Carole and Michael had a new baby, and Carole's business was taking off. Carole thought it could grow even bigger, so she needed to reach customers who lived further away – but how? She decided that the best way would be to produce a catalogue showing all the items she was selling. With a catalogue she could reach people all over the country. Customers could look through it, place an order and Carole could send them their party supplies through the post. It was a lot of work, but Carole had help, both from Michael and also from Catherine and Pippa, who she recruited to be models in the catalogue.

Spare Time

When Carole wasn't working and Catherine wasn't at school, Catherine and Pippa played with their friends from the village. They went on walks with their family in the countryside and did arts and crafts with their grandparents.

Catherine's grandmother Valerie was a skilled sewer and taught her how to make simple things. She also made Catherine costumes for fancy-dress parties.

Holidays with the Middletons

One of the things that inspired Carole's business was how much she enjoyed celebrating with her family. As the children grew bigger, so did their birthday parties. There were fancy-dress parties, pirate parties and water balloon fights. And it wasn't just birthdays – Easter and Christmas were a big deal too. Carole loved to bake, and her children loved to help her.

At Christmas, Catherine and Pippa helped their mother decorate the house, and also their bedrooms, with homemade decorations. They made cards to send, and a wreath for guests to admire when they arrived at the door.

The Middletons liked to be outdoors, and Christmas was no different. On Christmas Day, they would go on a long walk before coming home for their Christmas meal, and only after that would they open their presents.

When Catherine was off school for the holidays, she and her family liked to go hiking and camping in the English countryside, particularly the Lake District. Michael's work for British Airways meant that they were sometimes able to get discounts on flights, so the family went abroad whenever they could.

Doting Grandparents

Catherine's grandparents were always on hand to help look after her and her siblings and attend family celebrations. Carole's parents lived in a nearby village and Michael's parents lived a little further away in the next county.

Catherine's grandfather Peter, Michael's father, was a keen sailor and had his own sailing boat which he took Catherine and Pippa out on. He was good at woodwork too, so he built them their very own pirate ship to play on in their garden.

Happy Days

Catherine enjoyed school and threw herself into many different activities. She loved music and learned to play the flute, which she practised at home. When she was good enough, Catherine played the flute in the school orchestra and in a group of flute players called the Tootie-Flooties. Catherine liked to sing too, and performed with the school choir. The choir sang at church services and entered a BBC competition where they placed in the top fifty.

Catherine joined the school Brownie pack – the 1st St Andrew's. In the meetings, which were held after school, Catherine and her fellow Brownies took part in local community projects. She learned skills to earn badges, which her mother would sew onto her Brownie sash, worn over her yellow and brown uniform.

When Pippa turned five, she joined her sister at St Andrew's and eventually joined the Brownies too. Pippa was as energetic and enthusiastic as her sister and fitted right in, joining the sports teams and doing well in her lessons.

Catherine enjoyed playing on the school sports teams, and was selected to play for the hockey, netball and tennis sides. She enjoyed athletics too, and her school high-jump record is yet to be broken. The teams trained and played matches after school, which meant Catherine and Pippa often didn't get home until after six o'clock.

Even when Catherine wasn't on the pitch she liked to support her schoolmates when they played against other teams. One of these teams had a very famous player – Prince William! Catherine didn't meet William that day, but his presence at the school for a hockey match caused quite a stir.

Catherine took ballet and tap lessons, appeared on stage in recitals and acted in school plays. She was confident and keen to take on challenges such as public speaking competitions. Catherine's teachers were confident in her too, which is why they trusted her in lead roles in the school productions of the pantomime *Cinderella* and the musical *My Fair Lady*.

Catherine Marries a Prince

In one school production, Catherine played a young woman named Maria who married a prince called William. Sadly they didn't live happily ever after as the Prince William in the play murdered Maria and buried her body under a barn! Carole and Michael were in the audience to watch their girls perform whenever they could and stood at the side of the pitch watching their hockey matches. They were pleased to see how well their girls were doing and how they were growing up.

Moving On

In Catherine's final year at the school, the teachers made her a prefect, which meant she was responsible for helping some of the younger pupils understand the school rules. As well as being a prefect, Catherine won a special award for her sporting achievements at the school. Catherine turned thirteen in 1995, which meant it was time for her to leave St Andrew's. She'd loved being a pupil there so much that she wanted to come back when she was older and work as a teacher. Catherine didn't get to fulfil her dream of becoming a teacher but she did get to return to the school.

A Glimpse into the Future

Catherine revisited St Andrew's on St Andrew's Day in 2012, when she was invited to open a new hockey pitch. When she addressed the teachers and pupils, she got to demonstrate the public speaking skills she had learned at the school many years before.

"IT WAS WHILE I WAS HERE AT SCHOOL THAT

I REALIZED MY LOVE OF SPORT. SPORT HAS BEEN A HUGE PART OF MY LIFE, AND I FEEL INCREDIBLY GRATEFUL FOR THE OPPORTUNITIES I HAD TO GET OUTSIDE AND PLAY IN SUCH WONDERFUL OPEN SPACES."

Catherine, Princess of Wales, then Duchess of Cambridge, 2012

As Catherine's final term drew to a close, the Middletons had to decide where she should continue her education. They hoped their next choice would be as good for Catherine as St Andrew's had been. Sadly, it wasn't.

A PRINCE'S PROGRESS

On 15 January 1987, William, who usually insisted on choosing his own clothes, put on a smart white shirt, red tie, grey shorts and a grey-and-red cap. It was his first day at Wetherby School in Notting Hill, London.

While many children are nervous on their first day at school, William had more reason than most. When William arrived at the school, his mother told him that when they got out of the car, he would be met with a bank of photographers and that he needed to be on his best behaviour. The princess's bodyguard reported William's terse reply.

"DON'T LIKE 'TOGRAPHERS."

William, Prince of Wales, 1987

When they got out of the car, Diana held William's hand tightly to stop him from dashing past the photographers to get into the school. Instead he gave them a polite wave.

After his first day, Diana took William to school as often as she could, and collected him at the end of the day, often bringing a treat that she had picked up at the supermarket. Diana wanted both her sons' lives to be as normal as possible. She wanted them to mix with ordinary children and choose their own playmates, not be educated in a palace and only allowed to play with a list of pre-approved children. But she could not escape the fact that their lives were anything but normal.

The press had agreed to leave Diana and William alone when they travelled to and from school, but they did not. After his first day, William was keen to dash past them and see his friends. William liked school and got on well with the other boys. He played sports, including football, and took part in sports day. In 1989, Harry joined his brother at Wetherby.

William and his brother were both happy at school, but things were miserable at home. Charles and Diana argued a lot. Diana was often unhappy, and the media interest in her life made her feel paranoid and spied upon. William didn't like to see his mother upset. When she cried, he would push tissues underneath the bathroom door to dry her tears.

Charles began to spend more and more time at Highgrove, where William and Harry would travel with their nannies to join him at weekends.

At Highgrove, William and Harry had the run of the gardens. They could visit the farm, swim in the pool or fight battles in the tree house, but in the house itself, they had to be quiet. Charles was often working, holding meetings or hosting guests. Prince Charles's work was very important to him. He founded a number of charities and was a patron of many more. Charles's work would often mean he stayed in his office late into the night, sometimes falling asleep at his desk.

William Leaves Home

While his parents were living increasingly separate lives, William was about to break out on his own too. On 11 September 1990, William started a new school – Ludgrove in Berkshire. William's parents were there for his first day, but they had not travelled together. Instead they rode in separate cars, meeting up just before arriving at the school to make it appear they had been together all along. After posing for photographers and meeting with the headmaster, Diana and Charles again went their separate ways, leaving William at school.

Boarding school was a shock for eight-year-old William. He was used to sleeping in his own room near his brother's, and his nanny was always there when he needed her. At boarding school, he had to share a room with other boys.

William missed his home and his parents, and he worried about them too. He worried about his mother being unhappy, and about their fighting. William was protective of his mother and didn't like to see her frightened or upset. He said he wanted to become a police officer when he grew up, so he could make sure she was safe. His mother was often chased by photographers, even when she was driving her car. Sometimes they would shout at her and try to get her to react. He worried that she might get hurt without him there to protect her.

A Good Sport

Thankfully Ludgrove had a lot to keep William's mind and body occupied. The school encouraged its boys to do lots of sports. There were cricket pitches and a golf course as well as an indoor swimming pool. William was a natural athlete and soon made it onto the teams.

William saw his parents at weekends and during the holidays, but he would sometimes feel anxious when it was time to return to school. When Diana drove him back, she turned up the radio as loud as it would go and got him and his brother to sing along.

"YOU'D BE SINGING AND LISTENING TO THE MUSIC RIGHT THE WAY OUT INTO THE GATES OF SCHOOL, WHEN THEY DROPPED YOU OFF. AND THAT'S WHEN REALITY KIND OF SUNK IN THAT YOU REALLY WERE GOING BACK TO SCHOOL BECAUSE BEFORE THAT YOU'RE LOST IN SONGS."

William, Prince of Wales

William was right to be worried. Charles and Diana's fights were getting worse and their relationships with other people were harder to hide. Reporters followed them wherever they went and even intercepted their telephone calls, printing what they learned in the newspapers. Staff at the school did their best to keep the papers away from William, sometimes pretending that they hadn't been delivered, but they couldn't stop other pupils telling him what they'd heard from their parents when they went home.

William Goes Walkabout

William's very first walkabout took place when he was just eight years old. Princess Diana arranged for William to attend a service at Llandaff Cathedral in Cardiff, Wales, on 1 March 1991. That's an important day in Wales.

ST DAVID'S DAY

St David, the patron saint of Wales, is believed to have been born on the southwest coast of

Wales around the year 500 CE. David trained to become a priest in the Christian church. He was a successful priest, and was said to have founded twelve monasteries around Wales. A monastery is a community of men who have devoted their lives to Christianity by becoming monks.

One of the miracles David is said to have performed took place while he was preaching to a crowd in a village called Llanddewi Brefi. The crowd of eager listeners was so big that the people at the back were unable to see. David was said to have raised the land on which he stood to become a hill, so that everyone could get a good view of him.

St David is believed to have died on 1 March 589. On 1 March each year, people in Wales celebrate St David's Day by attending parades and wearing the Welsh national flower, the daffodil, on their clothing. Some people dress in Welsh national costume, which includes a tall black hat with a red cape. Women wear a white dress and men wear black trousers and a red waistcoat.

William wore a navy-blue suit with a daffodil pinned to the jacket lapel. He took part in a walkabout with his father and mother and met with men and women who had served with the armed forces. William shook hands with people in the crowd and pulled a lever to unveil a plaque.

It was a lot for a young boy, especially one whose parents couldn't agree, but William performed brilliantly. He had watched his mother and father greet people since he was a little boy, so he knew how to behave and put people at their ease. People in the crowd were delighted to see him.

WHAT IS A WALKABOUT?

A royal walkabout is when members of the royal family take time during their visits, or before or after big occasions such as weddings, funerals or jubilees, to meet people who have come to see them. While this might not seem like a big deal, it's not something members of the royal family have always done. Queen Elizabeth II was the first royal to perform walkabouts, on her tour of Australia and New Zealand in 1970. There, instead of waving to the crowds of people from an open-topped vehicle, Elizabeth opted to go on foot, giving her the opportunity to talk to people. During the first walkabouts, Elizabeth did not shake hands with people, but nowadays, members of the royal family are often seen shaking hands and accepting gifts of flowers.

Broken Crown

William enjoyed being at Ludgrove. There was a golf course and putting green where students could try their hands at golf. Of all the sports played at Ludgrove, you might think that golf wasn't one that sounded particularly dangerous, yet it was from the golf course on 4 June 1991 that William was rushed to hospital in an ambulance. One of William's friends hadn't been paying attention when he swung his club and brought it down on William's head, cutting it open. William's security officer travelled with him to the Royal Berkshire Hospital, where his parents rushed to be by his side. After being examined, William's doctor said that he had a fractured skull and needed surgery. For this, William would need to see a specialist. He travelled to Great Ormond Street Hospital, London, in an ambulance, with his mother by his side. William's surgery took over an hour. The surgeon was confident that it was something he could do easily and told Diana and Charles that there was no need for both of them to stay at the hospital. Diana didn't want to leave – she wanted to make sure William was okay. Charles, however, didn't stay. Having taken the doctor's advice, he left to keep an engagement at the opera and then travelled up to Yorkshire to an attend a conservation event.

Harry visited his brother the next day, by which time William was sitting up and full of stories about what had happened. William made a full recovery, though he was left with a scar on his forehead which would later give him something in common with another famous boy: Harry Potter.

Family Tour

In October 1991, William went on another walkabout, but this wasn't in England or even in Wales – it was on a royal tour, when he travelled with his mother, father and brother to Canada. While on tour, Charles and Diana's visits reflected their different interests. Charles called at local business initiatives, science laboratories and conservation areas, gave a talk to business leaders about environmental responsibility, and visited a mine, while Diana visited cancer patients in a hospital. As well as her official work, Diana took William and Harry on a trip to see Niagara Falls.

For William, who was still not very keen on photographers, it was a taste of what his future was going to look like when he finished his education. As a working royal he would be expected to make a certain number of visits on behalf of the queen, and when his grandmother died and his father became king, as Prince of Wales he would be expected to take on even more.

With his grandmother still in excellent health and his father far from old, it didn't seem likely that it would happen any time soon, but Charles and Diana and the queen wanted to make sure that when the time came for William to be king, he would be ready.

Different Paths

Even though they went on the same royal tour, attended the same schools and were born into the same family, William's future was very different from the life Harry could look forward to. As first-born son, William would one day inherit the throne. As much as his parents, like any other parents, tried to treat their sons equally and not favour one over the other, the brothers, through no fault of their own, were on very different paths. And other members of the family sometimes made it clear that they thought William was special. The Queen Mother would often invite William to visit her at Clarence House without his brother, and insisted that he sat next to her whenever they were together.

Broken beyond Repair

In March 1992, William was at the hospital again, but this time he was a visitor, not a patient. William was visiting his grandfather, his mother's father, Earl Spencer. He had suffered a stroke in 1978 and had never fully recovered his health. Then in 1992, Earl Spencer was admitted to hospital with a lung infection called pneumonia. Diana and William were going on a skiing holiday the next day and Diana wanted to make sure they saw her father before they left. Soon after their visit, Earl Spencer died of a heart attack, aged sixty-eight. Diana flew home as soon as she heard the news. Charles offered to travel with her, but she did not want him to.

Earl Spencer's death was a hard loss for William and Harry, and it was a tough start to what turned out to be a very difficult year.

Diana and Charles had drifted even further apart and life had become very hard for them and everyone around them. The disagreements that had happened in private were now out in the open. Stories appeared in the press about how little time they spent with one another, and who they were seeing when they weren't together. Diana and Charles, both keen to clear their names, leaked stories to the papers about each other's behaviour. Newspapers carried new stories about their private lives every day and journalists went to great lengths to get the latest scoop, following them and those close to them everywhere they went and intercepting their telephone conversations. People close to them were paid for the latest inside information.

Diana worried that she was being drowned out by Charles and Buckingham Palace's powerful press office. She wanted the chance to tell her side of the story and she did this with the help of a journalist named Andrew Morton. After they met, Diana agreed to let Andrew tell her story in a book. Rather than write it herself, or meet with him again, Diana agreed to record herself talking about her life and her marriage to Charles. Andrew Morton used these tapes to write a book. The book, *Diana: Her True Story*, was published in June 1992 and became a worldwide bestseller.

Red-Faced Royals

William was devastated by the book. He was embarrassed, not only by how his parents had behaved, but by the fact that his mother had chosen to talk about it, which meant that everybody knew the intimate details of her and Charles's private lives, and his too.

William wasn't the only one who was embarrassed. The queen had hoped that Charles and Diana could live separately and avoid a scandal, but this was not to be.

After a summer in which their parents had dominated the news, both William and Harry were happy to get back to school, but it wasn't long before they got a visit from their parents. Charles and Diana were there to tell them that they were making their separation official.

Diana was going to live at Kensington Palace, and Charles would split his time between Highgrove and Clarence House. They wanted to make sure William and Harry knew that although their parents would live separately, they loved their children very much and would work together to take good care of them.

Shortly after the visit, in December 1992, Prime Minister John Major read a statement in parliament from Buckingham Palace announcing Charles and Diana's separation.

"THIS DECISION HAS BEEN REACHED

AMICABLY AND THEY WILL BOTH CONTINUE TO PARTICIPATE FULLY IN THE UPBRINGING OF THEIR CHILDREN."

Prime Minister John Major

A Heavy Burden

William was protective of his mother and spoke to her on the telephone a lot. Diana relied on William to cheer her up and make her feel better. This was hard for William. He wanted to help his mother, but he was still a child and away at school. As much as he wanted to support Diana, her book and her behaviour were hurting him.

The announcement of his parents' separation meant that they were in the news yet again.

While William didn't like it, he hoped that the separation would put a stop to the stories and that they would both be happier and able to get on with their lives.

MIDDLETONS ON THE MOVE

Shortly after she left St Andrew's Preparatory School, Catherine and her family started packing up their home in Bradfield to move to a bigger house in the village of Bucklebury. Carole and Michael had made a lot of friends in Bradfield but their children were growing, as was the business, and they decided that they needed and could afford more space.

The new house had five bedrooms and a large garden, which included a tennis court. Carole and Michael bought some extra land around the house too, to extend the garden. Catherine was excited about the new house and her new bedroom, which her mother let her help decorate. This time, Catherine opted for paint rather than stickers and chose a tasteful pale blue and cream colour scheme, while Pippa opted for a more daring red.

Once they had moved into their new home,

the Middletons threw a big house-warming party for all their friends. As well as more space and a tennis court, the new house had something else to recommend it. It was only ten minutes away from Catherine's new school.

In September 1995, Catherine started her new school, Downe House. She was excited about this. She had enjoyed her time at St Andrew's and left loving her teachers as much as they loved her. Catherine hoped that Downe House would be the same.

Downe on Her Luck

Downe House was a private boarding school for girls aged eleven to eighteen. Most of the students boarded, which means they lived at the school during term time. However, as the school was so close to their new home, the Middletons decided that Catherine would be a day pupil, which meant she could go home after lessons were finished for the day.

Catherine worked hard at her lessons and tried to take part in school sports, just as she had done at St Andrew's, but there was a problem. There was no hockey at Downe House, the sport Catherine had excelled at. Instead, girls played lacrosse, and some of them were very good at it. Catherine had not played lacrosse before and so didn't make it onto the school team. She tried to make friends, but she didn't feel like she fitted in. Going home at the end of every day, she missed the evening activities and would have to learn about them the day after.

Not only that, Catherine joined the school when she was thirteen, and many of the girls had been there since they were eleven. Catherine tried, but found it hard to break into the friendship groups that were already established.

Catherine was miserable, and her parents were worried about her. Michael and Carole spoke to the head teacher, but unfortunately it didn't help. The Middletons also sought the advice of the head teacher at St Andrew's, who told them that Catherine might do better elsewhere. After visiting another new school, the Middletons agreed.

A Fresh Start

Rather than let Catherine finish the year, Michael and Carole pulled her out of Downe House after her second term and enrolled her in a school one hour away from their home called Marlborough College. This time, the Middletons decided it would be best for her to be a boarder.

After being so unhappy at her last school, Catherine was anxious about starting all over again and having to make new friends. Not only that, it was Catherine's first time staying away from home and the new routine was a lot to get used to. With the help of another pupil who was assigned to look after her and introduce her to other students, Catherine made friends quickly.

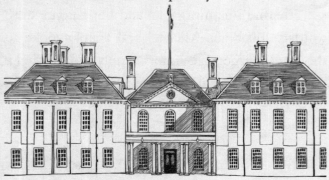

A Day in the Life at Marlborough

7.00 a.m. Wake up.

8.45 a.m. Start lessons.

1.00 p.m. Lunch.

2.00 p.m. Sport.

4.00 p.m. Lessons continue.

6.00 p.m. Supper.

7.30–9 p.m. Homework.

9.00–10.30 p.m. Free time. Watching television and listening to music.

10.30 p.m. Bedtime.

At St Andrew's, sport had played a big part in Catherine's life. At Marlborough, her skill on the hockey pitch soon earned her a place on the team. She also played netball, as goal attack, and tennis.

Since the school wasn't too far away, Catherine's parents were regular visitors. They came to see her compete against other teams but also to check that she was happy. They were delighted to see that she was.

When Catherine broke up for the summer holidays, she couldn't wait to get home to tell her sister about all the fun she was having and how much Pippa would like it when she started in September.

After the hard time Catherine had starting at Downe House, she kept a close eye on Pippa when she joined her at Marlborough. She wanted to make sure her sister had a better time than she did, but she needn't have worried. Pippa fitted in right away, she made the hockey team, did well in her classes and soon had her own pack of friends to hang out with.

And Pippa had her sister too, not only on the hockey team, but sometimes playing duets together at school concerts.

Teachers at the school could see that Catherine was responsible and friendly, and so she was given the job of helping to look after new students when they arrived at the school. This was the perfect job for Catherine, who knew how hard starting a new school could be. Even though Catherine got good grades and played for the first teams at sport, she was down-to-earth and approachable, and a good friend who young students could confide in when they missed home.

Juggling her responsibilities of schoolwork, looking after new students and playing for the school teams wasn't easy, but Catherine took it in her stride and in the summer term of 1998, she sat eleven GCSE exams.

After her exams, Catherine let her hair down. She'd worked hard and now she had a long and exciting summer to look forward to. First up was a trip with the school hockey and rugby teams to South America. There, Catherine's team competed against other schools and only lost two matches. It was the first time Catherine had travelled so far without her parents, and she enjoyed the independence. After the trip, the Middleton family went on holiday to the Caribbean.

It had been a summer filled with opportunity and fun, but Catherine was looking forward to getting back to school. Now Catherine was in the upper school, she had to wear a different uniform of a long black skirt with a fitted jacket. The boys dressed differently too, wearing suits. Whether it was her new uniform or the confidence she gained from travelling with the team, other students at the school started to notice Catherine. She had shiny long hair and a big smile, but Catherine didn't pay much attention – she was busy having fun with her friends.

Catherine also had her A-levels to study for – she took maths, English and art. When Catherine finished school, she knew she wanted to study history of art with a view to maybe working in a gallery one day, but she wasn't sure which university she wanted to attend. Even though she hadn't finally made up her mind, she applied to Edinburgh, where she would be able to study with some of her friends.

In Catherine's final year at school, her teachers made her a prefect. Prefects at Marlborough were expected to act as ambassadors for the school, which meant they had to speak to people about what made the school such a great place to be.

Catherine's school schedule was busy. She had sports, prefect responsibilities and her studies to keep on top of. Catherine wanted to do well and worked hard. When her A-level results arrived, she was pleased to see that her hard work had paid off. She earned two As and a B, more than enough to go to Edinburgh with her friends in September, but Catherine still wasn't sure that Edinburgh was where she wanted to go. She wanted more time and perhaps an adventure or two before she made up her mind.

A ROYAL TRAGEDY

Diana and Charles tried to keep life outside of school as normal as possible for William and Harry. The holidays would look different from now on, but Diana and Charles made their homes as welcoming as possible, displaying pictures of the family during happier times.

Life with Diana

When William and Harry spent time with their mother, she wanted to give them a chance to do what ordinary children did at weekends. She saw what palace life was like and felt her boys needed the chance to be silly now and then. To do this, she took them to theme parks and to fast-food restaurants.

She also wanted them to see just how privileged their lives were and show them how hard life could be for people who didn't have all their advantages. Diana took the boys to homeless charities to meet the people they served, and to visit people in hospital.

Diana was patron of a charity in London called Centrepoint that worked with people who were homeless to help get them off the street. Diana took her sons to Centrepoint to meet the people the charity served. It was something neither of her boys ever forgot.

"MY MOTHER INTRODUCED THAT SORT OF AREA TO ME A LONG TIME AGO. IT WAS A REAL EYE-OPENER AND I AM VERY GLAD SHE DID. IT HAS

BEEN SOMETHING I HAVE HELD CLOSE TO ME FOR A LONG TIME."

William, Prince of Wales

Life with Charles

When William and Harry stayed with Charles, things were very different. Charles had grown up immersed in palace life, so what might seem very strange to other people, such as hunting and shooting and moving from palace to palace, was entirely normal to him. When Charles was three, his mother became queen. The queen took her duties very seriously, which meant she was often away on tour, and had many engagements that required her time. Duty was important to Charles too. He felt it was his duty as Prince of Wales to use his position to help as many people as he possibly could.

As Charles often had to work when they came to stay, he hired a family friend, Tiggy Legge-Bourke, to look after the boys. Tiggy took them on hikes and hunts and made sure they got lots of fresh air.

Charles wanted his sons to grow up with the same sense of duty that he had. He believed that everyone, royal or not, had a duty to do their bit to make the world a better place. Charles believed there were lots of ways to do this, and one of them was picking up litter. When Charles took his boys out on walks, he would get them to pick up any litter they saw as they went, sometimes even picking up rubbish with spikes and putting it in rubbish bags. William and Harry thought this was how everyone went on walks and were surprised when they were teased for doing it on walks with their school friends.

William had hoped his parents' separation would put a stop to the embarrassing stories about them appearing in the newspapers, but it did not. If anything, things got worse when recordings of his parents' private telephone conversations were printed.

At Ludgrove, William was sheltered from the worst of it, but some stories were so big they could not help but get through.

Charles Gives an Interview

On 29 June 1994, Charles took part in an interview with a journalist named Jonathan Dimbleby. In the interview Charles talked about his childhood and his life with Diana. He also confessed that he was in love with Camilla Parker Bowles and had been during the time he and Diana were together. Charles wanted the interview to give people a chance to see a different side of him, but many decided they did not like what they saw. Charles also authorized Jonathan Dimbleby to write his biography, and gave him access to his many diaries and archive of letters.

The day after the interview aired on TV, the newspapers were filled with stories about Charles, some questioning whether someone who had behaved in such a way was fit to be king. Diana was embarrassed by the interview, and was concerned about how it would affect William and Harry. Diana travelled to Ludgrove to see them. She wanted to tell them that she was all right and explained that although she and their father loved them very much, they had found it impossible to live with each other. She also confirmed that what Charles had said about Camilla was true.

Rather than spend his time obsessing over his parents, William threw himself into school life and surrounded himself with friends he could trust – friends who would be there for him when he was down, and who would not tell stories about him. When William did suspect that someone was spreading gossip about him, he would stop being friends with them right away. But William would soon have to find a new group of friends. He turned thirteen in June 1995, which meant it was time for him to leave Ludgrove, a place where he'd been very happy.

William Goes to Eton

On 6 September 1995, William travelled with his father and mother for his first day at his new school, Eton College. Charles had wanted to attend Eton College himself when he was a boy, to be closer to his family at Windsor Castle. Diana's father and brother had gone to Eton, so she was familiar with the school and felt comfortable sending her boys there. Harry came with them so that he could get to know the place for when it was his turn.

WHAT IS ETON?

Eton College in Berkshire, England is the largest private boarding school in the country, and one of the most famous schools in the world. It is also very expensive. Parents of boys who attend Eton can expect to pay more than £45,000 a year.

Eton College was founded in 1440 by Henry VI. King Henry set aside seventy places for boys who did not come from wealthy backgrounds to give them the opportunity to get an excellent education. After attending the school, students were expected to take up places at a college he founded at Cambridge University – King's College, which opened in 1441.

People who have attended Eton are known as Old Etonians. They include twenty British prime ministers – including Boris Johnson and David Cameron – and the actors Eddie Redmayne and Tom Hiddleston.

Eton is famous for its distinctive uniform of a black tailcoat, worn with pinstriped trousers, a white shirt with a stiff collar and a white tie.

Living within the walls of the school, William felt safe from the press and could hide from the stories about his parents. Other students knew who he was, of course, but they soon got over it. William involved himself in the life of the school, once again excelling in sports. He took up water polo and proved to be an excellent swimmer, becoming captain of the swimming team. As captain, William was responsible for picking the team and helping to coach younger swimmers.

Visiting W.C.

On Sundays, William visited his grandmother at Windsor Castle to have tea and cake. William's favourite was chocolate biscuit cake, and the queen made sure that there was always some for him when he came. For Queen Elizabeth, it was a chance to get to know her grandson, and a chance for her to talk to him about what his life might be like when he became king. William did not tell his friends that he was going to tea with the queen so as not to draw attention to himself.

He just said he was going to W.C., which they knew stood for Windsor Castle.

Panorama

In November 1995, just two months after he started at Eton, Diana took part in her own television interview. Diana had been introduced to the journalist Martin Bashir by her brother, Charles Spencer. Bashir told Diana he had evidence that Charles and the palace were paying people to spy on her. He showed her bank statements to prove it. Bashir said that the interview, which would be aired on the BBC news programme *Panorama*, would be her chance to tell her story once and for all.

Before the interview was broadcast, Diana visited William at Eton to tell him what to expect. She said that she hoped William would be proud of her.

William watched the interview in his housemaster's office and was not proud at all. He was upset and embarrassed by the interview and was angry that once again that his parents' private lives were all over the news.

William was unhappy about Diana's interview for many years after it aired and he was even more upset when an investigation discovered that Martin Bashir had faked the evidence he had shown Diana to convince her to take part.

"THE INTERVIEW WAS A MAJOR CONTRIBUTION TO MAKING MY PARENTS' RELATIONSHIP WORSE, AND HAS SINCE HURT COUNTLESS OTHERS."

William, Prince of Wales, May 2021

A Royal Divorce

His mother's interview was too much for William. The stories in the papers increased and the press followed her wherever she went. William asked his parents not to come to school events because of the chaos it caused when the press arrived with them. The interview was too much for the queen too, and the wheels were set in motion for Diana and Charles to divorce once and for all.

Charles and Diana's divorce became final in August 1996. After much disagreement, Diana got to keep her title as Princess of Wales and her home at Kensington Palace.

Diana and Charles agreed that the boys would split their holidays between them. Charles enjoyed taking the boys skiing and to Balmoral and Sandringham. Diana took the boys on holidays with her friends.

In the summer of 1997, Diana took William and Harry on holiday to the South of France to spend time sailing on the yacht of her new friend Mohamed Al-Fayed. Mr Al-Fayed was very wealthy and owned a luxury store in London, named Harrods. Mohamed promised Diana that he would be able to keep the press away from her and her boys to give them a break.

William was glad to spend time with his mother and he hoped that the press would leave them alone. Unfortunately that was not to be. The British press found out where they were and managed to get pictures of Diana on board the yacht. Then more photographers arrived, laying siege to St Tropez.

The boys did their best to have fun playing on jet skis, but it wasn't the relaxed holiday they had looked forward to.

William and Harry left to spend the rest of the holiday with their father and to celebrate their great grandmother's ninety-seventh birthday. Charles took William and Harry on the Royal Yacht *Britannia* up to Scotland. It was the yacht's final voyage and a chance for the royal family to say goodbye to a ship that had been very important to them.

HMY *BRITANNIA*

Her Majesty's Yacht (HMY) *Britannia* was a 126-metre-long yacht commissioned by Prince William's great grandfather, King George VI, shortly before he died. The royal yacht was designed to allow the royal family to travel in comfort and receive important guests while away from home. *Britannia* was used for 968 state visits and travelled more than a million nautical miles. *Britannia* was the last of eighty-three royal yachts since the 1600s. William's father sailed on *Britannia*'s maiden voyage in 1954, from Portsmouth to Malta and on to meet his mother Queen Elizabeth in Tobruk, Libya. To keep the young prince and his sister, Princess Anne, entertained, the queen had the craft fitted with a slide, a sandpit and a pedal car in the shape of a yacht.

The royal yacht went out of service in December 1997 as the government were no longer willing to foot the bill to maintain it when more affordable and efficient means of transport were available.

Although the yacht is no longer used by the royal family, you can visit *Britannia* in Edinburgh.

The boys then travelled to Balmoral to spend their time with their father and grandparents. The boys were always busy at Balmoral, playing games or dashing about outside. They spoke to their mother when they could on the phone.

On Saturday 30 August, Diana called to speak to William and Harry. The boys were playing outside when they were asked to come in to talk to their mother. Neither of them stayed on long because they were keen to get back to their game. It would be the last time either of them ever spoke to her.

The Very Worst Day

The following morning William woke up early, as he did most mornings. He hadn't slept well, and shortly after he woke up, his father came into his room. Charles sat on William's bed and told him that his mother had been in a car accident in Paris, and that she had died. William was devastated.

Charles left to give Harry the same terrible news. The boys' lives would never be the same again. From all over the house they could hear the sound of crying as they hugged their father.

"IN THE DARK DAYS OF GRIEF THAT FOLLOWED, I FOUND COMFORT AND SOLACE IN THE

SCOTTISH OUTDOORS. AS A RESULT, THE CONNECTION I FEEL TO SCOTLAND WILL FOREVER RUN DEEP."

William, Prince of Wales

Charles arranged to fly out to France to bring home Diana's body. William and Harry would stay in Scotland with their grandparents and cousins. The queen felt that the boys needed privacy to come to terms with the news. Later that morning, they went to church near Balmoral. William felt that he could talk to his mum there, that he would somehow be closer to her in a church. The queen went with them.

"IT IS NOT LIKE MOST PEOPLE'S GRIEF, BECAUSE EVERYONE ELSE KNOWS ABOUT IT, EVERYONE KNOWS THE STORY, EVERYONE KNOWS HER."

William, Prince of Wales

And everyone did feel like they knew Diana. They had followed her life in the papers, which had printed stories about her almost every day for years. Her death was a shock for William and his brother, but it shocked the nation too. For their mother, although her life was over, her story was not. People watched the news to find out more about how she had died, to find out what the royal family's plans were. The journalists who had followed Diana every day now covered her death. Some blamed Charles and the royal family for how they treated Diana during the divorce. They felt that the queen should cut short her holiday at Balmoral and travel to London to pay her respects.

The queen felt she belonged with the boys and that they needed a chance to mourn in peace. But the pressure grew. Thousands of people travelled to Buckingham Palace to lay flowers and pay respects of their own. Tributes and messages of condolence poured in from all over the world.

"THEY LIKED HER, THEY LOVED HER, THEY REGARDED HER AS ONE OF THE PEOPLE. SHE

WAS THE PEOPLE'S PRINCESS AND THAT IS HOW SHE WILL STAY, HOW SHE WILL REMAIN IN OUR HEARTS AND OUR MEMORIES FOR EVER."

Prime Minister Tony Blair

The night before Diana's funeral people lined the streets, some in sleeping bags, just as they had the night before her wedding.

The Longest Walk

On 6 September, one week after receiving the tragic news, William and his brother dressed in black suits and black ties for their mother's funeral. In the royal family, it is a tradition for close family members to walk behind the coffin as part of the procession to Westminster Abbey. Even though William and Harry were just fifteen and twelve years old, their father believed that they should do the same. On top of Diana's coffin was a simple display of white flowers with a card that read "Mummy".

The funeral service at Westminster Abbey was watched by millions all over the world. Afterwards, William travelled with his father and brother to Althorp House in Northamptonshire, where Diana had spent her childhood. Diana was buried on an island in the middle of a lake. The path to the lake is lined with thirty-six oak trees, one for each year of her life.

Getting Away

After some time at Highgrove, friends of Charles invited the boys to stay with them in Botswana. It would be a chance for them to get away from the UK and the press. While there, they stayed on a conservation reserve which bred black rhinos to help prevent the species from becoming extinct. Though it was illegal to hunt black rhinos, they were hunted by poachers who could make a lot of money from selling their horns.

William loved the animals and the adventure and he loved not feeling like he was always being stared at. After the trip, William returned to school, where he could put on his uniform and do his best to blend in among the other boys. It had been the most terrible few months of his life.

The Prince and the Press

William saw the effect that the press had on his mother – they frightened her and they frightened him too. Many people blamed the press for Diana's death, including William's uncle, Earl Spencer. The earl believed that newspaper editors had Diana's blood on their hands for the way they had pursued her in the final years of her life. After Diana's death, an organization called the Press Complaints Commission drew up new guidelines to regulate how the press were allowed to report on people's private lives. It was hoped that the guidelines would make life easier for public figures like William and prevent what happened to his mother from happening again.

Wills Mania

Although William did not like the press and had no interest in posing for their pictures or answering their questions, the press were more interested in him than ever. At fifteen years old, Prince William had caught the eye of teenagers around the world. He was young, athletic, had good manners, and some thought he was very handsome. Magazines ran articles about William and featured fold-out posters of the young prince for fans to put on their walls.

In March 1998, Charles took William and Harry to Canada to go skiing. When they arrived in Vancouver, the cheering crowd made it very clear who they were there to see. William was greeted by thousands of screaming fans waving flowers and signs declaring their love for him. Back at home, the press referred to the reception as "Wills Mania".

Brothers Reunited

In September 1998, Harry joined his brother at Eton, but if Harry had hoped they would be partners in crime as they had been at Highgrove, he was disappointed. William had his own life at Eton, his own interests and his own friends.

Eton was William's home away from his family, so William asked Harry to leave him alone while he was there.

William did well at school, throwing himself into school life and making the most of everything Eton had to offer. He was captain of the swimming team and helped to train younger swimmers and pick members of the junior teams. In his final year William was invited to join a society known as Pop – an elite group of prefects. Members of Pop were allowed to wear waistcoats with different designs to the rest of the school. Some boys wore sequins or cartoon characters, while William opted for a patriotic Union Jack.

Moving On

William took his A-levels in the year 2000. He chose to take biology, geography and history of art. He had worked hard and hoped he had done well. School had been a big part of William's life, but while he was grateful for his time at Eton and the good friends he made there, he was ready to move on. William wanted to continue his studies at university, but first he wanted the chance to go on some adventures of his own.

CLOSING THE GAP

Both William and Catherine had decided to take what is known as a gap year before continuing their studies at university.

WHAT IS A GAP YEAR?

A gap year is a year-long break some students choose to take between finishing school and starting university. Some students use this time to earn money to help fund their studies. Others use the time to gain life skills and experience life outside formal education.

Catherine wasn't going to spend her year sitting in front of the television or twiddling her thumbs. She wanted to use the time to learn new things and see the world.

Catherine's first stop was Florence in Italy, to stay with a cousin who was studying there. Catherine enrolled herself in a three-month language course in the city. When Catherine wasn't studying, she spent her time visiting art museums around the city and seeing some of the many paintings she had learned about in school.

When Catherine's course ended she travelled back to Berkshire to spend Christmas with her family.

After the new year, Catherine headed off again, this time back to South America. Her destination was Chile and she travelled with an organization called Raleigh International.

WHAT IS RALEIGH INTERNATIONAL?

Raleigh International, originally known as Operation Drake, was a scheme started in 1978 by Charles, Prince of Wales (now King Charles III) and Colonel John Blashford-Snell. The purpose of Operation Drake was to give young people from different backgrounds the opportunity to explore the world by taking part in international expeditions. Charles hoped the trips would inspire young people to be adventurous, and think about ways they could change the world. Six years later, the project transformed into Operation Raleigh, which helped young people to volunteer on science-based projects such as surveying coral reefs in the Bahamas or doing geological surveys in Antarctica. While on expedition, young people learned independence and leadership skills. As well as the science projects, young people were expected to help on community initiatives, such as building schools and bridges.

In 1992, Operation Raleigh became Raleigh International and shifted its focus to projects that help conserve the environment.

The number of spaces on Operation Raleigh expeditions was limited and volunteers were chosen by interview at selection weekends where they also faced physical challenges.

In July 2022, Raleigh International's board of trustees decided to close the organization for good following two years of travel restrictions imposed to combat the spread of COVID-19 (see page 225). According to its website, before it closed, Raleigh International helped 55,000 young people contribute more than 100 million volunteer hours to projects in fifty countries around the world.

With her bag packed with waterproofs, warm clothes and a sleeping bag, Catherine flew to Chile at the end of January. She and the other volunteers in her group were given a couple of days to get over jetlag before they went on a trek through the mountains of Patagonia. After three weeks of trekking, Catherine and her group travelled to the coast, where they were trained to perform marine animal surveys, helping local scientists identify and count marine life. For the final part of her expedition, Catherine travelled inland to help build a fire station in a local community. It was an experience unlike anything she had done before. In the evenings she cooked for her fellow volunteers and played cards.

For the final part of her gap year, Catherine spent four months working as a deckhand on a yacht in Southampton. It was hard work – she began at 7 a.m., scrubbing the deck and hoisting the sails, and finished late in the evening, chatting to guests and topping up their drinks. She could then socialize with her crew mates before falling asleep in her cabin.

Great Minds Think Alike

When Catherine arrived in Chile to begin her gap year, she probably heard about a famous royal volunteer who had completed his expedition not long before she arrived.

William had chosen a similar expedition with Operation Raleigh. Like Catherine, he had flown to Santiago in Chile and travelled on to Patagonia, but unlike Catherine he could not travel with his fellow volunteers as he wanted, as he didn't want the press to know about the trip until it was well underway. Once William did arrive, however, he was treated the same as the rest of the volunteers in his team, getting over his jetlag while completing a few days of training in first aid and using a radio.

Once this was over, the team set out on an ocean trek in sea kayaks where they paddled through cold wind and battled high waves. At night they slept in tents, but when the wind was too strong they huddled together under waterproof sheeting. It was a far cry from his cosy study at Eton and even further away from Highgrove or Kensington Palace, but the extreme conditions helped the group to bond. People

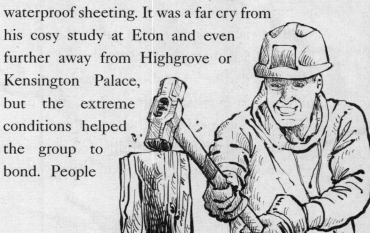

liked William because he proved himself to be hard-working and calm under pressure.

For the next part of his expedition, William travelled inland to a village where he and his team helped to build walkways so the local people could negotiate the steep terrain. Members of the team took turns to help out in the local village school. This was the part of the trip that William loved best, playing football with the kids and getting to be silly.

Throughout the trip, William had not been bothered by the press. People knew who he was and sometimes stared at him when he passed through, but he had much the same expedition experience as everyone else – although this came at a price. William had made a deal with the press – they would leave him alone if he would let them join him for a day in the village. He posed for photographs and allowed himself to be filmed as he went about his work, cooking, building and even scrubbing toilets. The press and the public loved what they saw. People were used to seeing the royal family shaking hands and cutting ribbons, but William was working hard and getting his hands dirty.

The final stage of William's expedition was the environmental project. The Chilean government and the Natural History Museum in London asked Raleigh International volunteers to help them study how loss of habitat had affected a species of deer called the huemul. The huemul deer was once common but had become endangered. William and his group helped to track the animals and studied their behaviour and movements.

Life on the Farm

When William returned home, his hard work continued when he took a job working on a farm owned by his friend's parents. William knew that he would one day inherit his father's Duchy of Cornwall estate, made up of many farms managed by tenant farmers. Charles wanted William to have first-hand experience of life on a farm so that he could understand some of the challenges faced by people who work in agriculture.

On the farm, William was expected to get up at 4 a.m. to move the cows to the milking sheds.

After that, William had to wash down the sheds ready for the next milking. William liked life on the farm – it was hard, but he liked being treated as one of the workers.

To Kenya

For the last few months of his gap year, William went to the Lewa Wildlife Conservancy in Kenya. He used some of the building skills he had learned on Operation Raleigh to make a wooden birdwatching hide. William's first attempt didn't go according to plan and sank deep into the swamp, but his second try was a success, and was used for years afterward.

"THE AFRICAN CONTINENT HOLDS A VERY SPECIAL PLACE IN MY HEART. IT IS

THE PLACE MY FATHER TOOK MY BROTHER AND ME SHORTLY AFTER OUR MOTHER PASSED ON."

William, Prince of Wales

One reason William loved Lewa was because it was far away from the press. Lewa was hard to get to, and William felt like he could be himself when he was there.

William chose his university for similar reasons.

Heading North

William's A-level results of an A, a B and a C – and the fact that he was the future king of England – meant that realistically he could have chosen any university he wanted. But William wanted the opportunity to have a normal university experience. He felt his best chance of that was at a university far away from London, or any major city.

UNIVERSITY OF ST ANDREWS

The University of St Andrews was founded in 1413. It's the oldest university in Scotland and the third oldest in the English-speaking world.

St Andrews is a small town on the east coast of Scotland. In 2001, the town had a population of just under seventeen thousand people. St Andrews is famous not only for its university

> but also for golf, as it is home to one of the most famous golf courses in the world.

St Andrews' location and small population made it the ideal place for William to go to university, because he could hope for some privacy from the press. When the palace announced that William would be attending St Andrews, applications went up by 44 per cent!

In September 2001, William travelled up to Scotland with his father. Before going to the university, the Palace arranged visits for William and Charles. Charles's press officer said that they were using the trip as an opportunity for Charles to introduce William to more of Scotland.

Glasgow

William and his father visited a housing estate in Glasgow called Sighthill on 21 September 2001, to boost morale and to see if any of Charles's charities would be able to help the community. A year earlier, asylum seekers from troubled countries around the world had been given homes in the area. Some people already living in Sighthill were not happy to have asylum seekers move into their community. Some did not believe the community had enough resources to be able to support the new residents as well as the people who already lived there, and others were suspicious of the new people. The newcomers did not feel welcome, and many didn't feel safe. On 5 August 2001, a twenty-five year-old Kurdish refugee named Firsat Dag was murdered while on his way home from a night out. Following his death, hundreds of asylum seekers and their supporters had marched to Glasgow to attend a vigil for Firsat and demand better conditions and protection.

While visiting Sighthill, William and his father watched a performance by a local dance group and visited a group of elderly people who met regularly in the local community centre.

Wherever they went, they were met with crowds of people eager to meet nineteen-year-old William. Many of his fans were young women and girls who screamed as if they were at a rock concert, but some of them were a little older – Dorothy Gordon, a member of the local pensioners' group, spoke to William and even managed to get his autograph!

"IT WAS A GREAT DAY. WILLIAM SPENT SOME TIME TALKING TO US ALL. HE WAS VERY DOWN-TO-EARTH. I HAVE A PICTURE OF HIM UP IN MY LIVING ROOM TO REMIND ME OF THAT FANTASTIC DAY."

Dorothy Gordon

Following their visit to Sighthill, William and Charles paid a visit to the US Consulate in Edinburgh, where they signed a book of condolence for the terrorist attacks that had taken place in the United States ten days earlier.

11 SEPTEMBER 2001

On 11 September 2001, nineteen men hijacked four passenger aeroplanes and used them in an organized terrorist attack on targets in the United States. The hijackers crashed two planes into the Twin Towers of the World Trade Center in New York City, one into the Pentagon, Washington DC, and the fourth came down in Pennsylvania. The attack claimed the lives of nearly three thousand people. A terrorist group named al-Qaeda claimed responsibility.

William arrived at his new university on 23 September, where he was greeted by a familiar crowd of adoring fans. He looked embarrassed but managed to pose for some photographs before making his way into St Salvator's Halls, his new home. Charles followed, carrying his suitcase. As with William's schooldays, the palace had agreed that the press would give him space while he was a student.

St Salvator's Halls, or "Sallies" as it is known to students, was built in the 1930s to house the university's growing population. Most students at St Andrews choose to live in university accommodation for their first year, before moving into privately rented housing for the rest of their time.

William had a room to himself, but shared the kitchen and bathroom with other students. There was a food hall, but at weekends, students had to either get takeaways or make food for themselves. St Salvator's had a dining room where the students could eat during the week. There was also a common room with table tennis and pool tables, a fireplace and a piano. Luckily for William, a few friends from Eton were also residents in the hall so he soon found he had a group of people he could trust to have fun with. This was important for William, who sometimes found it hard to know whether people wanted to be friends with him because they liked him or because he was a prince.

A Lot in Common

After turning down her place at Edinburgh, Catherine applied to study at St Andrews and was accepted. Catherine arrived more than a week before William, as did most of the first years, to take part in something known as Freshers Week. Many universities host Freshers Weeks for new students, to give them a chance to get to know one another and find their way around before their courses begin.

Shortly after Catherine arrived, she and the other first years listened to a talk from the university principal. He encouraged all the new students to work hard at their studies but also to have fun getting to know one another. He said that St Andrews had the reputation for being a place where people met their future husbands and wives. But if Kate had looked around at her fellow students, she wouldn't have seen her future husband – because he hadn't arrived yet.

A few weeks after William got to St Andrews, he and his friends became more aware of a girl with long brown hair who fellow hallmates referred to as "Beautiful Kate". Intrigued, William invited Catherine to join him and his friends for breakfast in the dining room. As they talked, they realized they had a lot in common, including some friends and the fact they were both studying history of art. They talked about their Raleigh International expeditions and what they hoped to cover on their course. Catherine was naturally friendly and easy to talk to and soon became a part of William's group of friends, going to parties and hanging out at the bars in town.

Student Life

After the adventures of her gap year, Catherine was keen to study again and threw herself into her work. Catherine took good notes during her lectures which she happily shared with

William whenever he couldn't attend. With their shared course, and halls and friends in common, Catherine and William were seen together a lot. Some people made jokes about them liking one another, but others were less kind. Some students, who had applied to St Andrews with the purpose of meeting William, were jealous of Catherine and said mean things about her. Catherine didn't like this as it reminded her of her miserable time at Downe House.

But it wasn't all studying and mean girls. There was plenty of fun too, including a big shaving-foam fight during a traditional celebration called Raisin Monday.

In November of their first year, Catherine and her friends auditioned to take part in a charity fashion show as models. The fashion show would take place in spring and raise money for breast cancer and childhood diabetes charities. Catherine was keen to experience everything university had to offer.

William didn't take part. While he liked having a good time, he didn't want to be photographed doing anything wild enough to get him on the front page of next day's papers. Also, he found the attention he got from some female students could be hard work.

Some girls even changed their courses to be closer to him. William had to stay very quiet about anyone he liked and be careful when he went out on dates. As soon as the press suspected he was interested in someone, the young woman in question would be followed by journalists and photographers and pressured to answer questions about him. They would question her family too, and anyone she had ever been friends with. William knew that unless he was very serious about someone, it wasn't fair to put them through that.

William did join the water polo team and auditioned to be in a production with the drama society. He did well in the audition, but didn't get the part. The society felt that if William was cast it would turn their small performance into a media circus.

William had wanted to have the same experience as the other students, but he couldn't. Wherever he went in town he felt like people were staring, and some over-eager students would interrupt his conversations in their efforts to make friends with him. At the end of his first term, he wasn't sure he wanted to stay.

Over the Christmas holiday, William discussed how he was feeling with his father. Charles had also had a tough time settling down when he went to Cambridge, and told his son that he hoped he would stick it out. William agreed to give it another chance. He'd made good friends and hoped that perhaps changing his course might make things more interesting for him, so he switched from history of art to geography. At school William had enjoyed studying geography and got top marks in his A-level.

When they returned in January, William was much happier in his new course, and Catherine got some exciting news too. She had been selected to take part in the charity fashion show. It was going to be a big event. Journalists wanted to know whether St Andrews' most famous student would be there.

Kate Takes to the Catwalk

Catherine was soon busy with rehearsals and fittings and learning how to walk the catwalk. The show featured some big designers. As a model, Catherine had a table for her friends close to the front, and William had a place.

Catherine was scheduled to wear a number of outfits, one of which was a sheer dress which she was meant to wear with a sweater. Kate thought it looked better without the jumper and the organizer of the show agreed, so Kate walked the catwalk in a very daring design.

When the excitement of the show was over, Catherine and her friends, including William, went on to an after-party. Whether because of seeing Catherine on the catwalk or the excitement of the whole evening, after the fashion show, William and Catherine became a couple.

TOGETHER AGAIN

At the end of term, Catherine and William went their separate ways for the summer, secure in the knowledge that they would see a lot of one another when they returned. Catherine and William had agreed to share a flat in town with two of their friends for their second year.

The flat, on Hope Street, had two storeys and plenty of space for entertaining. Before they could move in, police officers needed to make sure that the prince would be safe there. They installed bombproof doors and fitted bulletproof shutters on the windows. The residents on Hope Street were also vetted, and warned that a very important resident would soon live close by.

When they returned to St Andrews in September, the flat was ready. Catherine decorated her room with photos of her family and her travels.

Life in the flat was different to being in halls. They had to make all their own meals for a start. William, Catherine and their flatmates often made dinner together and invited friends to join them for dinner parties. Catherine and her friend Olivia took charge of the cooking, and William and Fergus handled going to the local supermarket to get supplies.

In the flat, William and his friends could relax and have fun without worrying about tales being leaked to the press. Outside was a different story. Whenever William walked around the town with a female friend, people and the press speculated whether she could be his girlfriend.

William and Catherine could be together among friends, but never held hands in public in order not to draw attention to themselves. They were careful to appear as though they were nothing more than flatmates and friends.

Away from the flat and when she wasn't studying, Catherine had a lot of interests. She was a member of an all-women's society, the Lumsden Club, that organized charity events. As well as this she worked as a waitress and played for the university hockey team.

Tired of being watched around town, William liked to stay home and socialize with his flatmates and trusted friends, watching movies and eating takeaways.

Living together gave William and Catherine the chance to get to know each other better without the world outside watching. As they got closer, they realized they liked each other very much.

Party Perfect

In January 2003, Catherine turned twenty-one and her family threw her a big party at their home in Bucklebury. Catherine decided to have a 1920s theme and invited friends from school and university, and of course William. The party was held in her parents' large garden, where Michael and Carole had hired a big tent called a marquee and arranged for a band to play and for food to be served. It was the first time they had hosted royalty in their home, but Catherine had a wonderful time and was glad to see all her friends together.

As Catherine had invited William to her

twenty-first celebration, it seemed fitting that William invited her to his. Like Catherine's birthday, William's was hosted by his family at one of their homes, but this home was Windsor Castle and William's family included his father, Prince Charles, and his grandmother, Queen Elizabeth II.

Things Get Wild at Windsor

On his birthday, William gave an interview to the press in which he claimed that he was single. He said it was hard for him to date because he didn't like how the press treated women he was interested in, following them and quizzing them and their families. William knew what he was talking about, as a reporter had already attempted to interview Michael Middleton about his daughter's new friend.

William's birthday party had a theme too – he had chosen Africa and asked his guests to dress up with this in mind. As his guests arrived at the castle, there was one who had not been invited. When a comedian named Aaron Barschak arrived, he was moved along by police. But he didn't give up – he walked away from the police and climbed over the castle wall. Once inside the grounds, Barschak found his way into the building and persuaded a member of staff that he was a guest who had become lost. The member of staff led Barschak into the party, where he was able to run onto the stage and kiss William. For a moment William thought it was a prank organized by his brother, but it wasn't.

Luckily Barschak was just a comedian, who didn't want to do anybody any harm, but he could have been someone with worse motives. Barschak was arrested and removed from the party. After the party, the royal family asked for an investigation into how the security services could have allowed them to be put in such a potentially dangerous situation.

A House in the Country

When William and Catherine returned to university in September 2003, they didn't go back to the flat they had shared on Hope Street.

Instead they and two of their friends rented a large house outside town, set in a beautiful garden surrounded by high walls. They had picnics in the garden and hosted their friends for dinner.

It was the perfect place for them to get away from busy university life and the chaos that sometimes surrounded William.

Catherine needed a place to get away too. While the summer had been filled with birthday parties, it had also been tinged with sadness as her grandfather, Ron Goldsmith, passed away. Ron had been ill for some time, but Catherine had been close to him and his death still came as a shock to her and her family.

Catherine had always worked hard at school and university was no different. She paid attention in her lectures and was determined to get good grades.

Catherine had told her family that she and William were seeing one another. Their close friends knew and kept their secret, but it couldn't stay under wraps forever.

Going Public

In April 2004, the couple's private life became public when William invited Catherine to join him and a group of his friends skiing at Klosters in Switzerland. Klosters was the royal family's favourite ski resort and William had been many times, but Catherine was a new companion. While they rode the chairlift up the mountain, a photographer took a picture.

The picture was printed in the *Sun* newspaper. The Palace refused to confirm or deny whether William and Catherine were a couple and claimed that the newspaper had breached the agreement they made to leave William alone while he was at university. The newspaper argued that William was a public figure and away from university, so he was fair game.

Back at St Andrews, Catherine and William were more careful than ever. They did their best not to be seen together while they were out and about. At weekends they drove to Balmoral and stayed together at a cottage on the estate.

They were very much together, but William

worried that they might be too young to be so settled and so serious. He knew his future as heir to the throne would be filled with duty and responsibilities and this was his time to have fun. William and Catherine agreed to take some time apart over the summer to think about whether they wanted to be so committed.

Catherine returned home to Bucklebury with her family. She got a job with a local clothes shop, but it wasn't easy for her to stay focused on work. Because of the picture at Klosters, the press wanted to know more about her and her relationship with William. Curious people also came to the store, pretending to be interested in clothes, but really to see what she was like. The store manager said that Catherine took it in her stride but it made her day difficult. She also travelled to France and stayed with friends.

William travelled too – to America, and then to Greece with some friends of his own. It was a time for them both to think about whether being together was really what they wanted.

Coming Home

In September, William and Catherine returned to St Andrews and settled back into their lives together. This was the beginning of their fourth and final year at university. The work they did this year would be their last chance to earn marks towards their final grade. Catherine wrote an extended essay, a dissertation, on *Alice's Adventures in Wonderland*. Catherine had chosen a subject that interested her and wanted to do well. Unlike William, whose future was decided from the moment he was born, Catherine would need to find a job after graduating. Getting a good degree would give her a wider range of opportunities. William did his extended project on the effect of dynamite fishing on the coral reefs of the island of Rodrigues, a place William had visited and scuba dived before. Their university days would soon be over and their lives would change forever.

A Son's Blessing

William's life was about to change in another way. When William saw his father over the Christmas holidays, Charles asked him for his blessing to marry Camilla. William hadn't always liked Camilla. Growing up, his mother spoke about how Camilla's relationship with Charles made her very unhappy, and both William and Harry found this hard to forgive. But as years passed, William saw how happy Camilla made Charles and how well they worked as a team. With his son's blessing, Charles asked Camilla to marry him in December 2004 and she accepted.

After their summer break, Catherine and William were very much together again and William included her in family occasions such as his father's fifty-sixth birthday party at Highgrove. In order not to arouse too much suspicion, Catherine and William did not arrive at or leave these events together, but the fact that she was included showed she was very much a part of his life. William's father could see that too, and he invited Catherine to join

William and the royal family in Klosters for his pre-wedding skiing party.

Though his father was ready to settle down and marry again, William was not and said so to a journalist while out partying in the ski town.

"I AM TOO YOUNG TO MARRY AT MY AGE. I DON'T WANT TO GET MARRIED UNTIL I'M AT LEAST 28 OR MAYBE 30."

William, Prince of Wales

But what William said to the journalist was very different to the way he was behaving. He and Catherine had been together for nearly three years and they had both met one another's families and were guests at each other's special occasions.

Wedding Bells

On 9 April 2005, Charles, Prince of Wales, married Camilla Parker Bowles at Windsor Guildhall surrounded by close family members and friends. William and Tom Parker Bowles, Camilla's son, stood beside their parents as witnesses. After the ceremony, the couple travelled to St George's Chapel, Windsor, to have their marriage blessed in front of 800 guests, including Queen Elizabeth and Prince Philip, and of course William and Harry.

The Final Test

Back at university, William and Catherine had to sit their final exams. A lot of the work they'd done over the previous three years counted towards their final grade, but William and Catherine still wanted to do well.

When their exams were over, Catherine and William celebrated with their friends, at balls organized for the final-year students and parties at their house. While other students' futures would be affected by their grades, William's would not – but he still wanted to get a good result. William and Catherine were relieved when they found out they'd both received upper second-class degrees.

A Graduation to Remember

William and Catherine were pleased with their results and so were their families, who attended their graduation ceremony on 23 June 2005.

It was a big day for both of them in more ways than one, because along with William's father, the queen and Prince Philip also came to the graduation. Kate had met the queen before, but this would be the first time she was able to introduce her to her parents.

It had been an important four years for Catherine and William, and they were four years William was very grateful for. Although his university life hadn't been completely standard, he had felt free enough at St Andrews to make good friends and to find Catherine. Outside the graduation hall, a crowd gathered to congratulate

William and he thanked them for allowing him to have such a fulfilling experience.

"I HAVE BEEN ABLE TO LEAD AS NORMAL A STUDENT LIFE AS I COULD HAVE HOPED FOR AND I AM VERY GRATEFUL TO EVERYONE, PARTICULARLY THE LOCALS, WHO HAVE HELPED MAKE THIS HAPPEN."

William, Prince of Wales

William and Catherine packed up the home they had shared for two years and said goodbye to St Andrews and their friends. To celebrate their graduation, they took a holiday together in Kenya, but when it was over, Catherine returned home to Bucklebury, and William took his first steps into his future life as an adult royal. With university and graduation behind them, both William and Catherine could look forward to a bright future, but they couldn't know whether they would be able to make a future together.

FACING THE FUTURE

William had enjoyed his time at university, but while some of the skills he learned might come in handy, he had grown up knowing who he was going to work for. As a member of the royal family and future heir to the throne, William was going to work for his grandmother, Queen Elizabeth II, the United Kingdom and the Commonwealth Realms. William moved into an apartment at Clarence House in London with his brother Harry.

Prince on Tour

One of the tasks William was expected to undertake was to go on official visits to the Commonwealth. In July he travelled to New Zealand for an official visit on behalf of the queen. As part of the visit, William represented the queen at ceremonies commemorating sixty years since the end of the Second World War, and planted a tree at Government House to represent the royal family's connection with the country.

William was also in New Zealand to support the British and Irish Lions rugby team. He had been invited by the team's head coach to give the players a boost and add a sense of occasion to their games. William had played rugby at school, so it was a thrill for him to take part in a training session with the team. He was popular with the crowd and gave some of the young fans a high five as he walked by.

The Patron Prince

As well as tours, William started choosing the charities he wanted to support as patron. His interest in rugby made one patronage an easy decision – in 2007 he became Vice Royal Patron of the Welsh Rugby Union, because he would one day be Prince of Wales. His brother Harry took the same post for the English Rugby Union. In these roles, the brothers could raise the profile of the game and help raise money to support initiatives to get young people involved.

WHY HAVE A ROYAL PATRON?

Organizations ask members of the royal family to represent them because having a royal on board raises the organization's profile. When a member of the royal family attends a charity's event or visits one of their projects, it's more likely to be covered by the press. The royals are also known for helping charities to raise more money for the cause they represent.

Royal patrons often know other informed and important people and so can connect a charity with other help they might need. A royal patron can also help a newer charity become more established.

In September 2005, the charity Centrepoint invited William to visit to see the work they were doing and meet some of the people they served. William volunteered with the charity for three days and liked what he saw. He remembered visiting Centrepoint with his mother when he was a boy and knew how much it meant to her. Seeing the work they were doing made him want to help in any way he could.

A Royal in the Real World

As well as his royal work, it was important for William to experience work done by ordinary people. The palace organized placements for him in industries including banking, healthcare and farming. William even spent time working on a fish stall at Billingsgate fish market in London. He spent time with the emergency services, joining an RAF helicopter search-and-rescue team in Anglesey. One placement his father was particularly keen on was shadowing an employee at the Duchy of Cornwall. Charles had taken over running the estate when he was twenty-one years old and used the money it brought in to provide for himself and his family, and to fund some of his charity work. When Charles became monarch, the title of Duke of Cornwall and the Duchy would pass to William. Charles wanted William to have a good understanding of how the estate worked before it became time for him to manage it.

WHAT IS THE DUCHY OF CORNWALL?

The Duchy of Cornwall is an estate owned by the Duke of Cornwall which is dotted across twenty-three counties in England and Wales. The Duchy makes money from the rent paid by people living in properties on its estate, and by taking a share of the profits made by the farmers who work some of the 53,000 hectares of land.

Officer Wales Reports for Duty

It's a tradition for male members of the royal family to spend time serving with the armed forces. William's father had served with the Royal Air Force and the Royal Navy. His grandfather, Prince Philip, had been an officer in the Royal

Navy during the Second World War. William's brother, Harry, had joined the army not long after he left school and was training at the Royal Military Academy at Sandhurst in Berkshire.

For William, it was especially important because one day he would be king and head of the armed forces – those serving would have to pledge an oath to fight for "king and country". Not long after his graduation, William spent four days undergoing rigorous tests to qualify for army officer training at the Royal Military Academy, Sandhurst. These included a physical fitness test, a medical examination and a psychological evaluation to make sure he was army material. William passed with flying colours.

WHAT IS THE ROYAL MILITARY TRAINING ACADEMY?

The Royal Military Training Academy, Sandhurst, is where men and women learn the skills they need to become officers in the

British Army. Officer training lasts forty-four weeks, broken down into three terms. Trainees at Sandhurst are taught basic military decision-making and leadership skills, and take part in challenging military exercises to test their abilities.

On 8 January 2006, William sat in the car as his father drove him to Sandhurst. Training was hard. Recruits had to get up early, take part in fitness training and perform repetitive drills. And the rules were strict – William learned to iron his uniform, keep his quarters tidy, make his bed and polish his boots and buttons until they gleamed. Creased shirts, scuffed boots and unmade beds resulted in a loud telling-off and being forced to do press-ups in front of the other cadets. William got no special treatment and very little sleep. Military exercises included twenty-four hour marches with heavy packs, and spending many nights sleeping outdoors in the field. Like the other recruits, William wasn't allowed to leave Sandhurst for the first five weeks. He had limited access to his phone and little contact with Catherine. But while there were many press-ups, the security of the base meant there was no press!

Chelsea Girl

Catherine also moved to London after leaving St Andrews. She lived in a flat bought for her by her parents on the King's Road in Chelsea, close to Clarence House, where she would visit William whenever he was home. Catherine shared the flat with friends and it was her parents' plan that Pippa would move in with her when she finished her studies.

Unlike William, Catherine's life was not mapped out for her. She moved to London hoping to find work, but despite her good degree and many important contacts, it wasn't easy.

Although they both moved to London, Catherine and William's lives looked very different, not only from one another's but from the one they had shared while they were students. At St Andrews they had lived together and spent as much time together as they wanted, but now it was more difficult, not only because of William's busy schedule, but also because of the press.

While William was a student, the press agreed to leave him alone. Now he had graduated, this agreement was over. William's new life meant he needed the press to report on the work he was doing for charity and for the country. The press were happy to do this, but it came at a steep price. Covering William's work meant they felt they were allowed to cover his private life too. William had a security team to help him manage this, but Catherine did not.

Life for Catherine became very difficult and sometimes dangerous. When she was with William she was protected, but when she wasn't with him and trying to go about her day – getting on buses, going out for dinner or to a bar with friends – the press followed her wherever she went. They waited outside her home and attempted to interview her friends and family. Catherine did not give any interviews or comment on her relationship, and she asked her friends to do the same. She did everything she could to ignore the attention, but when one paper published a picture showing her address, she knew they had gone too far.

William worried about Catherine. He didn't think it was fair that she should be treated this way because of him. William had seen how photographers had hounded his mother and made her life a nightmare. He didn't want the same thing to happen to another woman he loved. William's lawyers agreed to represent Catherine too and wrote to the newspapers on her behalf to ask them to leave her alone. His press secretary also worked with Catherine, giving her advice on how to behave. Catherine was given better security and had panic buttons installed in her apartment so she could call the police for urgent help if she felt threatened.

A Proud Day

In December 2006, William took part in a military ceremony, similar to a graduation, called a passing out. William's father and stepmother watched proudly. Catherine and her family were also there. William's grandmother was there too, but she wasn't sitting and watching. In the passing out ceremony, William had to march with his fellow new officers past the queen. Queen Elizabeth then inspected the new officers, speaking to some and smiling broadly at her grandson, before giving a speech.

William's family were very proud of him and how hard he had worked. Catherine was proud too, but it hadn't been an easy time for her. While William was busy at Sandhurst, Kate's life had been on hold.

Waity Katy

Catherine worked as an accessories buyer at a clothing retailer named Jigsaw. She had to travel to find inspiration and put looks together. This was an ideal role for art-loving Catherine. She loved fashion and had helped her parents launch a clothing line with their company, Party Pieces. But while it was an ideal role, it was not an ideal situation. Catherine's profile meant that the press would not leave her alone. She was followed as she drove to work, photographed when she walked inside, and television crews waited outside for her to leave at the end of the day. Her employers were understanding, they knew it wasn't Catherine's fault. They tried to help by letting her work flexibly and leave from other exits, but Catherine knew that if she didn't give photographers a picture, they would only follow her until she did.

When Catherine awoke on the morning of her twenty-fifth birthday in January 2007, she found a pack of photographers and press outside her flat, and as she drove to work, she was trailed by more than fifty paparazzi.

A spokesperson released a statement on William's behalf asking the press to leave her alone.

"PRINCE WILLIAM IS VERY UNHAPPY AT THE PAPARAZZI HARASSMENT

OF HIS GIRLFRIEND.
HE WANTS MORE THAN
ANYTHING FOR IT TO STOP.
MISS MIDDLETON SHOULD,
LIKE ANY OTHER PRIVATE
INDIVIDUAL, BE ABLE TO
GO ABOUT HER EVERYDAY
BUSINESS WITHOUT THIS
KIND OF INTRUSION. THE
SITUATION IS PROVING
UNBEARABLE FOR ALL
THOSE CONCERNED."

Buckingham Palace

But it didn't stop. Catherine wasn't just the subject of articles inside the newspapers and magazines, she was now on the front page. Something needed to change.

A Simple Solution

The answer to William and Kate's problem seemed easy – they should marry. The press nicknamed Catherine "Waity Katy". They claimed that she was impatient for William to propose and wrote articles about when and where their wedding would be held and what the public could expect from their new princess.

But it was all too fast for William. He felt that he was too young to marry. William knew how hard marriage could be for people in his family. His mother and father's marriage had ended in divorce, as had those of aunts and uncles.

The Break-Up

Feeling they had no other option, after four years together, Catherine and William agreed to separate at the beginning of April 2007.

Catherine was unhappy about the break-up. She loved William and wanted to be with him, but she also wanted a life. Their relationship had taken up a lot of her time since she started university. Now that she didn't have William to consider, Catherine was free to do whatever she wanted with her time. But how would she spend it? Catherine wasn't sure, but she knew she didn't want to waste it worrying about what William was up to.

Catherine joined a charity dragon boat crew. The crew was made up of young female athletes. Catherine and the crew trained regularly on the River Thames at 6.30 a.m. She wasn't an elite athlete but she was fit and had always been sporty, playing tennis and swimming regularly. Catherine enjoyed getting to know her teammates.

DRAGON BOAT RACING

Dragon boat racing originated in Southern China over two thousand years ago. A drummer in each boat kept the rowers in time. The race was thought to be lucky and to encourage a good harvest. Today, dragon boat racing is one of the fastest-growing water sports in the world. Each dragon boat holds a crew of up to twenty rowers who paddle for over 250 metres to the beat of their drummer.

After the break-up, Catherine accepted many invitations she might have turned down while she was with William – to gallery openings, luxury product launches, fashion shows, even a roller disco. When they were together, William often preferred to stay home to avoid the press, and even when they did go out, they had to avoid being photographed together. Now single, Catherine was still photographed, but she didn't have to worry about how it would affect William's future or the monarchy. But the pictures did affect William.

William's life was military training, royal duties and the occasional night out with friends. Seeing Catherine in the papers was hard. She seemed to be carefree and having the time of her life. He couldn't help but be reminded of the joy she had brought to his life. William knew he wanted her back.

William called Catherine and told her how he felt. After many phone calls and meetings to discuss how things would be different, they decided to get back together. Although they told their closest friends, they kept it a secret from the press.

Remembering a Princess

On 1 July 2007, Princes William and Harry marked what would have been their mother's forty-sixth birthday with a charity concert in her honour at Wembley Stadium. After welcoming the audience and paying tribute to their mum, William and Harry returned to their seats to enjoy the six-hour musical extravaganza. There were performances from artists Elton John, Lily Allen and Pharrell Williams and appearances from celebrities such as David Beckham. William danced next to his brother, while Catherine danced with friends two rows behind. While they weren't sitting next to one another, the fact that she had been invited made the press suspect the couple were back together.

Aiming High

Relieved to be reunited with Catherine, William continued with his military service. In January 2008, he reported for duty at Royal Airforce Cranwell in Lincolnshire to train as a pilot. William's father, Charles, had begun his service with the RAF and his grandfather, Philip, was also a keen pilot. At Cranwell William learned to fly different types of aircraft, starting with light aircraft all the way up to a Typhoon jet fighter. Training was tough. As well as flying, William had to spend many hours in the classrooms at Cranwell learning about the planes and how to use their many instruments. There were exams too, but William was used to those, and he passed.

On 11 April 2008, William was presented with his wings by his father at his RAF graduation ceremony while Catherine sat in the audience with her mother and William's family.

"IT WAS AN AMAZING FEELING."

William, Prince of Wales

Flying into a Warzone

When William began his military service, he wanted to be treated in the same way as other soldiers and serve on the front line, but he was not allowed. Military intelligence officers worried that William's position as future heir to the throne would make him a high-profile target for the enemy, and put the lives of the servicemen and women who served alongside him in unnecessary danger.

On 30 April 2008, William was given permission to fly in secret to Afghanistan to complete a very important mission. William was sent to boost the morale of the troops serving in Kandahar. He spent three hours at the base, meeting the troops before he had to fly back. But William's mission wasn't over – he had also been sent to bring home the body of a twenty-two-year-old British soldier who had been killed in the fighting. When he returned to the United Kingdom, William met with the soldier's family and told them how honoured he was to have been able to fly their son home.

THE WAR IN AFGHANISTAN

Following the terrorist attacks on the United States on 11 September 2001 (see page 136), a terrorist organization named al-Qaeda claimed responsibility. The hijackers had all trained in Afghanistan, and the United States government believed that the leader of al-Qaeda, a man named Osama bin Laden, lived in the country and was being protected by the leaders of Afghanistan, known as the Taliban.

In October 2001, the USA and its allies, including the UK, entered Afghanistan to fight al-Qaeda and the Taliban and find Osama bin Laden. The Taliban government fell quickly, though its forces spread throughout the region and continued to fight for many years. Osama bin Laden found a hiding place in neighbouring Pakistan. He was killed by US forces in 2011. The USA and the North Atlantic Treaty Organization (NATO) withdrew from Afghanistan in 2021.

Continuing His Service

Military life suited William. He liked being treated like one of the group and not a prince. In the military, William didn't have to worry about the press and he felt he was doing something useful. He wasn't ready for that to end.

William knew he would never be able to serve on the front line like his brother, but he still wanted to put the skills he had learned to use. He remembered his work experience with a search-and-rescue team and how much he had enjoyed it, and he thought it might be a way to use his pilot training.

Search-and-rescue work requires a great deal of skill. Everyone from the crew to the people being rescued relies on the pilot's instincts to keep them safe. While William had already received some training, to become a rescue pilot he would need a lot more – first at Cranwell and then at RAF Shawbury to learn to fly helicopters.

Brothers in Arms

Not long after William started his training, Harry joined him to train to fly defence helicopters. William had to spend many hours learning how helicopters work. The brothers helped each other with their studies, but there was time for fun too.

William and Harry shared a house and enjoyed living together again, though in an interview William joked that Harry was messy and snored loudly.

William in Wales

In January 2010, William moved to the island of Anglesey off the northwest coast of Wales for advanced helicopter training. To work in search and rescue, pilots need to be able fly in challenging circumstances, from gale-force winds over high seas to dense cloud over mountain ranges. They need to understand their complex instruments so they know, even in dark or foggy conditions, how high they are and in which direction they're flying.

Once William had mastered the basic techniques, he was ready to accompany RAF teams on real search-and-rescue missions and watch how it was done.

When William was sent to train in Anglesey, Catherine went with him. After their break-up, William and Catherine realized that if they were going to make it work, they needed to be together as much as possible. Anglesey was the perfect place for William and Catherine. They found a pretty four-bedroomed house with beautiful views and its own private beach. As Anglesey was an island with a small community, William and Catherine could live normally without being disturbed, just as they had in St Andrews.

William qualified as a search-and-rescue pilot in September 2010. He'd worked hard and was glad to find something he enjoyed doing that was truly useful.

"EVERY DAY YOU COME INTO WORK, YOU DON'T QUITE KNOW WHAT'S GOING TO HAPPEN. IT'S QUITE EXCITING

IN THAT SENSE, IT'S UNPREDICTABLE. BUT AT THE SAME TIME, IT'S GREAT THAT YOU GET TO GO OUT AND ACTUALLY SAVE SOMEONE'S LIFE, HOPEFULLY, OR AT LEAST MAKE A DIFFERENCE TO SOMEBODY WHEN YOU GET THERE."

William, Prince of Wales

William worked in a team of four, taking it in turns with other teams to be on call-out duty. When on call, he slept at the base. When a call for help came in, William and his crew would get ready and be on their way in as little as fifteen minutes, out to sea to rescue the crew of a capsized fishing boat or up into the mountains to find a lost hiker who had misjudged the weather. Conditions were often challenging, with strong winds, thick cloud, high waves and rough terrain. William had to use all his training to get his team to the rescue site safely, and once there, he had to use all his experience to keep his nerve.

Home, Sweet Home

When William finished his shift he would go home to the house he shared with Catherine. In 2010, he decided to ask Catherine to marry him, but he wanted it to be special. First he needed to choose a ring. For William it was an easy choice – the diamond and sapphire engagement ring his father had given to his mother. But where would he propose? William knew just the place.

THE DUKE AND DUCHESS OF CAMBRIDGE

With the ring stowed in his backpack, William flew with Catherine to Kenya. One evening at a lodge, miles from anywhere, he proposed to Catherine, and she said yes. Catherine was delighted, but they agreed to keep it a secret until they got home.

When they returned home, William and Catherine told their families. Both families were delighted by the news. Harry in particular was thrilled to be getting a sister. He liked Catherine very much and had become close to her.

On 16 November 2010, Clarence House sent out a statement to the press.

"The Prince of Wales is delighted to announce the engagement of Prince William to Miss Catherine Middleton. The wedding will take place in the spring or summer of 2011."

With the announcement official, William and Catherine gave an interview at St James's Palace. Catherine was nervous. She wore a blue silk dress that matched her sapphire ring perfectly.

William said he chose his mother's ring because he wanted a way for Diana to be a part of their future together.

"I THOUGHT IT WAS QUITE NICE BECAUSE OBVIOUSLY SHE'S NOT GOING TO BE AROUND TO SHARE ANY OF THE FUN AND EXCITEMENT OF IT ALL — THIS WAS MY

WAY OF KEEPING HER SORT OF CLOSE."

William, Prince of Wales

Decisions, Decisions

After the announcement, Catherine and William's lives became a whirlwind. As William was a member of the royal family, and second in line to the throne, their wedding would be a national event and would require meticulous planning. Thankfully they didn't have to do it all themselves – they had a whole team to help them. First they needed a location and a date. William and Kate decided on Westminster Abbey, and after consulting the palace and the government, they chose 29 April. This gave them just over five months to work on the arrangements.

When people get married, they receive presents from their guests. To make sure they don't get a lot of the same thing, many couples make a wedding list of items the couple would be glad to receive as gifts, such as things they'd find useful for their home. As William and Catherine already had a home, they didn't really need anything, but they knew that many people would want to give them something to celebrate their happy day. Rather than let people waste money on things they didn't need, Catherine and William selected twenty-six charities that were important to them, and set up a wedding gift fund. People who wanted to buy them a gift were instead asked to donate money to the fund. The fund was a great success and raised more than a million pounds for the chosen charities.

Say Yes to the Dress

Catherine also needed to decide who she wanted to design her wedding dress. The wedding would be watched by millions of people around the world, so not only did Catherine want to look wonderful, she also wanted to use the occasion to showcase British designers. Catherine chose an English designer named Sarah Burton, who worked for Alexander McQueen. It was an important job and staff at the fashion house had to keep every element of the design a secret until the big day. The dress was made of ivory satin covered in handmade lace featuring flowers from around the United Kingdom – roses for England, daffodils for Wales, shamrocks for Northern Ireland and thistles for Scotland.

Tiara Time

Nothing says "princess" more than a tiara, and Catherine had plenty to choose from in the queen's collection. Catherine originally said she wanted to wear a simple crown made of flowers, but seeing as her wedding was going to be far from simple, she chose a diamond tiara, known as the Cartier Halo tiara, instead. The Cartier Halo tiara was made for Queen Elizabeth's mother in 1936, from more than 850 diamonds.

Wedding Party

Catherine chose her sister, Pippa, to be her

chief bridesmaid. Pippa was there to support Catherine, help with her dress and to lead the younger bridesmaids up the aisle.

William chose his brother Harry to stand with him as he waited for Catherine to arrive and to look after the wedding rings. William chose two close school friends to give speeches after the ceremony. William did not want to make them his official best men as he knew that giving their names to the press would bring them a lot of unwanted attention.

A Royal Rolls

Catherine also had to decide how she wanted to get to the abbey. There were plenty of carriages and cars to choose from. Catherine felt that a princess would arrive at her wedding in a carriage pulled by horses, but she wasn't a princess yet. Instead she chose a Rolls Royce Phantom car. Catherine chose the Rolls Royce because it had large windows, so people would be able to see her sitting next to her father as they passed by.

When William and Catherine left the abbey,

Kate would be a royal, and so they decided to ride in the same carriage that had carried William's father and mother to Buckingham Palace after their wedding. This state landau was open, so Catherine and William could see and be seen by the people who lined the streets from the abbey to Buckingham Palace.

At Buckingham Palace, more crowds waited for them to arrive and to see them when they came out on the balcony with the rest of the royal family. When they did emerge, the crowds erupted. William was taken aback when he saw them.

"OH, WOW!"

William, Prince of Wales

The crowd called out for the happy couple to kiss. William and Catherine gladly obliged, not once but twice.

Having given the crowd what they came for, it was time for the reception. William and

Catherine invited 650 people to celebrate with them at Buckingham Palace, where they enjoyed champagne and canapés and an eight-tiered wedding cake.

Catherine and William's wedding had been a wonderful occasion for the happy couple and the royal family. Journalists wrote articles about how the young couple would breathe new life into the monarchy. The wedding was watched by an estimated audience of two billion people worldwide and became the most watched televised event in history.

Returning to Duty

After the wedding, rather than going on honeymoon, William and Catherine returned to their home in Anglesey, where William had to go back to work as a rescue pilot.

In many ways, life after they were married returned to the way it had always been, but for Catherine, her life had changed forever. While Catherine had been a commoner before she was married, she was now the Duchess of Cambridge and the future queen consort, and with these titles came a lot of responsibilities. Like William, Catherine was expected to perform royal duties on behalf of the queen and to select charities she would like to support and work with.

Catherine was given a secretary to help her to navigate her next steps. The secretary drew up a list of charities for her to choose from. Catherine particularly wanted to work with children's organizations, and as a former Brownie, she chose to represent the Scout Association. She also wanted the chance to use what she had learned studying history of art and so chose the National Portrait Gallery in London.

Royal Rules

Catherine had a lot to learn. Being a member of the royal family was very different to being a member of the Middleton family. There were rules about who she had to curtsy to, and when, and these rules changed depending on whether she was with William or was alone. There were other rules about how she was expected to dress for family occasions and how to behave on royal visits. Thankfully she had William and the rest of his family to help her.

Catherine in Canada

In June 2011, the Duke and Duchess of Cambridge boarded a flight to Canada to begin a nine-day official visit.

Packing for a royal tour had been very different to packing for a holiday. Catherine knew her picture would be taken wherever she went. She would need the right clothes for every event, from hospital visits to state banquets. Catherine worked with designers and her assistant to help her put together a wardrobe. For the tour, Kate chose to showcase a combination of British and Canadian designers. She wanted her style to be young but classic, and she also wanted to be more accessible than previous royals and combine expensive designer items with clothes bought from high-street shops.

William and Catherine were working twelve-hour days, travelling from place to place, with barely a moment to catch their breath. Everywhere they went they were expected to smile, be polite and make conversation. They laid a wreath at a war memorial in Ontario and visited Quebec and Prince Edward Island.

The events drew big crowds of people, keen to see the newlyweds. It was a fast tour with many stops, but wherever they went, the crowds showed up to greet them. Catherine took it all in her stride.

A New Home

When the tour was over, William and Catherine returned to Anglesey. While William continued with the search and rescue, Catherine got to work designing their new home. As their work often required them to be in London, William and Catherine needed somewhere to live in the city. William had shared an apartment at St James's Palace with his brother, but now he was married he needed a place where he and Catherine could start a family. The queen suggested an apartment in Kensington Palace. Having grown up in a different apartment there, William knew Kensington Palace well, and Catherine liked it too. Until it was ready, the queen granted them use of a small house nearby, called Nottingham Cottage.

It was a special time for William and Catherine as their duties were light. William knew that this wouldn't last forever. His grandmother, though still very active, was getting older. Neither she nor Prince Philip would be able to perform the many roles expected of them forever. This meant that other family members would need to step in and attend events, perform official duties and embark on tours on their behalf.

The year 2012 was a big year for the United Kingdom and for the royal family. In the summer, Queen Elizabeth II celebrated her Diamond Jubilee, marking sixty years since she came to the throne. The occasion was celebrated with street parties, concerts and firework displays, as well as a pageant on the River Thames in London. The queen led the way from Chelsea to London Bridge on the royal barge, and was followed by a flotilla of more than a thousand boats.

The 2012 London Olympic Games

Catherine and William and other members of the family attended many of the jubilee events, but it was a busy summer, because London was also hosting the 2012 Summer Olympic Games.

It was the first time London had hosted the Games since 1948. Preparations had been underway since 2005, when London's bid was announced as the winner by the International

Olympic Committee. The preparations included building new sporting venues around the country and a huge new athletics stadium in Stratford, London.

As the youngest and fittest members of the royal family, Catherine, William and his brother Harry were asked to be Olympic ambassadors. In this role, Catherine got to watch many of the competitions and take part in training with some of the teams. It was a dream for her to spend the day training with the British women's hockey team, who went on to win the bronze medal.

A Happy Secret

In the winter of 2012, Catherine and William found out they were expecting a baby. They were excited to become parents, but they wanted to keep the news to themselves for as long as possible. In the first weeks of her pregnancy, Catherine felt sick a lot. This is common, and Catherine hoped it would get better as time passed, as it did for most women. Unfortunately, rather than feeling better, Catherine felt much worse. She was sick so often that she struggled to eat and drink enough. After speaking to her doctor, Catherine was admitted to hospital at the beginning of December 2003, suffering from a condition called *hyperemesis gravidarum*, which is severe sickness in pregnancy.

Going into hospital meant that Catherine and William could no longer keep the news of the pregnancy to themselves, so William instructed his team to announce that Catherine was expecting a baby. William's own family only found out shortly before the announcement. The news caused so much excitement that Catherine and William's official website crashed due to the amount of traffic it received.

In hospital, Catherine was given fluids and medication. William visited her every day. Catherine soon started to feel better, but when she left hospital, she was advised to rest.

As Catherine's pregnancy progressed, excitement grew as to whether they would have a boy or a girl and what they would choose to call the baby.

THE SUCCESSION TO THE CROWN ACT 2013

Kate and William's child would become the first royal heir in the United Kingdom to be affected by a new act of parliament. The Succession to the Crown Act meant that William's oldest child would be his heir, whether they were a boy or a girl. Before the act was passed, the oldest son would have been William's heir, even if he had an older sister. A girl could only be heir if she had no brothers. Work to change this law began many years before it finally passed because it had to be agreed by all the realms of the Commonwealth.

A Right Royal Delivery

On 22 July 2013, Catherine and William welcomed a son into the world at St Mary's Hospital in Paddington, London. Shortly after the baby was born, William called his grandmother first, and then spoke to his father and brother. Everyone was delighted by the news.

The birth of William had been announced by a notice posted outside Buckingham Palace, but this time the news was delivered by the Duke and Duchess's press secretary just before 8.30 p.m. to make sure it could appear in the newspapers the next morning. The notice of the happy news was later posted outside the palace, just as it had for William.

As soon as the news was announced, congratulations poured in from friends, family, celebrities, world leaders and ordinary people all over the world. The proud parents received a lot of messages, via email and social media and through the post. The bells of Westminster Abbey rang in celebration and the fountains of Trafalgar Square as well as many other important buildings were lit up in blue.

Catherine and William spent the night with their new baby in the hospital before leaving the next evening, but not without giving the press the chance to get their very first pictures of the new family.

They were both very happy.

"IT'S VERY EMOTIONAL, IT'S SUCH A SPECIAL TIME. I THINK ANY PARENT WILL KNOW WHAT THIS FEELING IS LIKE."

Catherine, Princess of Wales,
then Duchess of Cambridge

After carefully putting the baby into a car seat, William drove Catherine and their son back to Nottingham Cottage to start their lives as a family of three. On 24 July 2013, William and Kate announced that their little boy was named George Alexander Louis.

William and Catherine had some decisions to make about what kind of parents they'd like to be. William's work as a search-and-rescue pilot meant not only long hours away from home, but also living far away from both their families. William was close to his father, but made no secret of the fact that he wished he'd been able to spend more time with him growing up. Charles's royal duties and commitment to his royal patronages had meant that he was often not around. William wanted his son to have a different childhood.

A GROWING FAMILY

In September 2013, William announced that his time in the military was coming to an end. William wanted to spend more time with Catherine and George, and his father and grandmother also expected him to take more of a role in their family too.

It was a busy life. William and Catherine hired nannies to help them balance their work and caring for their little boy, but they took him with them whenever they could.

George on Tour

In April 2014, Prince George followed in his father's footsteps by embarking on his very first royal tour with his parents. William and Catherine took seven-month-old George with them on a busy tour of Australia and New Zealand.

George was a hit with the crowds. While on

tour, he was presented with stuffed animals including a bilby – a rabbit-like desert creature – and an enormous wombat. At Taronga Zoo in Sydney, George was also introduced to a real wombat, who was named after him.

More Happy News

In September 2014, Catherine was due to make a solo trip to Malta, but doctors advised her to send William in her place. Catherine was sad to cancel, but delighted that she would soon be having another baby. As with her first pregnancy, Catherine suffered from severe sickness and needed medical treatment. Once her doctors had her condition under control, Catherine went back to work. She attended awards ceremonies and paid a three-day official visit to New York City, USA, where she visited a child development centre.

In February 2015, William left for Japan and China for a four-day visit, but Catherine didn't go with him as she was advised not to travel. William was the first member of the royal family to visit China in more than thirty years.

In March 2015, William announced that he was going back to work. He missed being a search-and-rescue pilot and so trained to become a helicopter pilot for the East Anglian Air Ambulance service. To commute easily to work, William and Catherine moved into a large house on the Sandringham Estate called Anmer Hall. Anmer Hall was surrounded by fields and countryside and would be the perfect place for the growing family to get away from the city and enjoy the fresh air. William had to complete a lot of training and sat fourteen exams to qualify, but he was delighted to get back into a helicopter and start work.

"THE MOMENT I STARTED THE HELICOPTER TRAINING, I REALIZED THAT IT WAS BETTER THAN ANYTHING. IT WAS ONE OF THOSE THINGS THAT I JUST INSTANTLY TOOK TO AND THOUGHT, 'THIS IS REALLY COOL.' I REALLY ENJOY IT."

William, Prince of Wales

Working as an emergency responder was difficult. William and his crew arrived at tragic scenes and had to try to help people going through some of the worst experiences of their lives. William said what he saw deeply affected him.

"SOMETHING THAT I NOTICED FROM MY BRIEF SPELL FLYING THE AIR AMBULANCE WITH THE TEAM IS, WHEN YOU SEE SO MUCH DEATH AND SO MUCH BEREAVEMENT, IT DOES IMPACT HOW YOU SEE THE WORLD.

I STARTED FEELING THINGS THAT I HAVE NEVER FELT BEFORE, AND I GOT VERY SAD, AND VERY DOWN."

William, Prince of Wales

William said seeing so much death and tragedy at work stayed with him for a long time and made him worry about similar things happening to people he loved.

A Little Princess

On 2 May 2015, Catherine gave birth to her second child, Princess Charlotte Elizabeth Diana. William took family leave from his job with the air ambulance to spend time with

Catherine, George and Charlotte.

For Charlotte, the fountains of Trafalgar Square and important buildings around London were lit up in pink.

Fun with the Grandparents

Now a family of four, William and Kate's lives were full to bursting. Thankfully they had their families to help them. Kate tried to see her parents Carole and Michael as much as she could and travelled to stay with them often. Carole loved spending time with her grandchildren. Charles enjoyed being a grandfather too. When George and Charlotte came to visit, he liked to read to them and to put on the voices of the various characters in the story. For George, Charles planted a garden at his home in Aberdeenshire and named it George's Wood.

Long Lived the Queen

In September 2015, Queen Elizabeth II became the United Kingdom's longest-reigning monarch.

She was eighty-nine years old and Prince Philip was ninety-four. While they were both still in good health, they weren't able to perform as many of their duties as before, and Charles often stepped up to take their place. Catherine and William took over some of their patronages too.

With moving house, a new job and the new baby, a lot had changed for William and Catherine, and there was a lot of change on the horizon for the country too.

In 2016 the British government asked people to take part in a special vote called a referendum. They wanted people to decide whether the United Kingdom should remain part of an organization called the European Union.

In February, Prince William made a speech to the Foreign Office honouring young diplomats in the service. In his speech, William praised the United Kingdom's ability to work with other countries and seek out new allies.

"IN AN INCREASINGLY TURBULENT WORLD,

OUR ABILITY TO UNITE IN COMMON ACTION WITH OTHER NATIONS IS ESSENTIAL. IT IS THE BEDROCK OF OUR SECURITY AND PROSPERITY."

William, Prince of Wales

For many who heard William speak, he was making clear his feelings against leaving the European Union. Some criticized William, saying that as a member of the royal family, he was not meant to give his view or attempt to influence other people's.

Working Together

Since William left university, he had shared what's known as a "royal household" with his brother Harry. A royal household is a department of staff who work to manage the schedule and correspondence of royal family members. Before William graduated, his work and duties were managed by his father's household, but as he took on more of his own work, Queen Elizabeth granted William and Harry a household to share at St James's Palace. When William married Catherine, it made sense for her to join that household.

Heads Together

William, Kate and Harry all supported different charities that reflected their interests. William worked on homelessness and bereavement charities, Catherine worked with organizations focused on early childhood and Harry worked with military charities that supported ex-service personnel. One thing that united all these causes was the topic of mental health and how important it is for people to feel they can openly discuss their struggles.

In May 2016, William, Catherine and Harry put their collective support behind a campaign called Heads Together. The campaign's aim was to unite some of the biggest mental health charities to help change the conversation about mental health, and tackle the stigma associated with mental health problems.

As part of the campaign, William and Catherine interviewed celebrities including Lady Gaga, Stephen Fry and Adwoa Aboah about their mental health and how talking about it had helped them when they were in a bad place.

A Reluctant Royal?

After the birth of Charlotte, both William and Catherine faced criticism for not taking on more royal duties. The press claimed that this was because they were lazy and "work shy". William was aware of the criticism, but he didn't take it too seriously. He was determined to spend time with his family and serve in his role with the air ambulance. William wanted to be there to guide his children in ways his own father had not.

> "I TAKE MY DUTIES AND MY RESPONSIBILITIES TO MY FAMILY VERY SERIOUSLY. AND I WANT TO BRING MY CHILDREN UP AS GOOD PEOPLE."

William, Prince of Wales

William's grandmother, the queen, may have been ninety years old, but she was still very active and unwilling to slow down. William said as soon as the queen wanted to give him more responsibility, he would gladly accept it, but until then, his place was with his family and the ambulance service.

Going Royal Full Time

In May 2017, after 22,000 solo visits and countless more beside his wife the queen, the Palace announced that Prince Philip was retiring. He had supported and served alongside the queen for seventy years, but had been struggling with his health for some time. Retiring meant that Philip would need to hand over many of his patronages to younger members of the family. William was needed now more than ever and, as promised, he eagerly accepted the call.

In July 2017, William announced that he was stepping away from the air ambulance service to take up royal duties full time. As well as this, William and Catherine were moving from their home in Norfolk back to Kensington Palace. Living in London would mean they were closer to Buckingham Palace and would be able to travel around the country more easily.

When Harry Met Meghan

Harry took up some extra duties too, but that wasn't the biggest change taking place in his life. On 27 November 2017, the Palace announced that Harry was getting married to an American actor named Meghan Markle. Harry met Meghan in 2016. They liked each other immediately and, after a whirlwind romance of little over a year, got engaged. When Harry introduced William and Catherine to

Meghan early in their relationship, the two couples got on well. William and Kate were delighted by the news that Harry was getting married.

"IT HAS BEEN WONDERFUL GETTING TO KNOW MEGHAN AND TO SEE HOW HAPPY SHE AND HARRY ARE TOGETHER."

William and Catherine

Once Harry was married, the queen promised him the use of Nottingham Cottage, close to Catherine and William in Kensington Palace. Harry hoped getting married would bring them all closer together. He loved being an uncle to George and Charlotte and looked forward to meeting their new sibling, due in the spring.

MEGHAN MARKLE

Meghan Markle grew up in Los Angeles, California, in the USA. Her mother, Doria, is an African-American yoga instructor and therapist, and her white father, Thomas Markle, worked behind the scenes in television. Meghan's parents separated when she was six years old and she split her time between each of their homes. After leaving school, Meghan attended Northwestern University in Illinois, before becoming an actor. Meghan was first cast in small roles in television programmes, but eventually appeared in films and in a starring role in a successful TV series that ran for nine seasons.

But Harry's relationship with Meghan did not bring him closer to his brother. In fact, as the day of the wedding approached, there were stories circulating that the two couples weren't getting on at all. As the rumours grew, the press made it clear they were on Catherine and William's side. The stories labelled Meghan demanding and rude. They claimed she made Catherine, who was pregnant, cry during a disagreement about Princess Charlotte's bridesmaid dress. The palace did not comment on the stories.

Both couples appeared to put their differences aside to celebrate the birth of Prince Louis on 23 April 2018. A month later, at Harry and Meghan's wedding, William stood beside his brother as his best man.

DIFFERENT PATHS

William and Catherine celebrated Christmas 2019 with the queen and members of the royal family. Queen Elizabeth invited William and George to help her make the traditional Christmas pudding.

Christmas at Sandringham had long been a family tradition for William and his family.

They arrived on Christmas Eve and often played a game of football against the staff. Presents were opened after dinner on Christmas Eve. On Christmas morning the family attended a service at the local church, but there was something different this year. Harry and Meghan were not there. They had decided to spend Christmas in Canada with Meghan's mother, Doria.

A Bad Start to a Terrible Year

In January 2020, Harry and Meghan – the Duke and Duchess of Sussex – announced that they were stepping away from the royal family. Harry had discussed his plans with William and his father, and while various options were considered, Harry felt he had no choice but to move aside.

"WE INTEND TO STEP BACK AS 'SENIOR' MEMBERS OF THE ROYAL

FAMILY AND WORK TO BECOME FINANCIALLY INDEPENDENT, WHILE CONTINUING TO FULLY SUPPORT HER MAJESTY THE QUEEN."

The Duke and Duchess of Sussex

After spending a short time in Canada, Harry and Meghan bought a house in California, USA. To become financially independent, Harry and Meghan signed a deal with a media organization to produce television programmes, including a series about how they felt they were treated by the British media and the royal family.

This was bad news for the royal family, but there was worse news to come – news that would affect everyone and change the world.

A World-Changing Virus

In January 2020, stories about a new virus, first discovered in Wuhan, China, in 2019, began appearing on the news. This virus was named COVID-19 and was spreading quickly. The symptoms of COVID-19 included a fever, cough and losing the senses of taste and smell. Some people with COVID-19 had no symptoms at all, while others became very ill, and some died. The worst symptoms were experienced by older people and those who had health conditions that made them more vulnerable to infection.

As the days passed, more and more people became infected. The government advised people to stop the spread of the virus by washing their hands and by staying two metres away from others. But the advice wasn't enough and the death toll began to rise. The government feared that if the spread was allowed to continue, hospitals would soon be overwhelmed. To ease the pressure, the government closed businesses and schools, implementing lockdowns to restrict where people could travel and limit their contact with others.

On 23 March 2020, Prime Minister Boris Johnson called on people to help prevent the spread of the virus by staying at home. New rules meant that people were only allowed to leave their homes to shop for necessities, exercise, seek or provide care, or travel to and from work. People were not allowed to meet with friends or family members they didn't live with. All non-essential workplaces and schools were closed.

The Cambridges in Lockdown

The lockdown affected everyone including William, Catherine and their three children, who all moved from Kensington Palace back to Anmer Hall in Norfolk. Like children all over the country, George and Charlotte's schools were closed. William and Catherine's many engagements were cancelled or moved online. They were lucky in that they had staff to help them, but things were still difficult. Catherine and William might not have been able to travel but they were still very busy with their various charities, staying in regular contact with them to find out how COVID-19 affected their work and the people they served.

Every Mind Matters

The lockdowns slowed the spread of the virus, but they were having a devastating effect on people's mental health. Lockdowns prevented people from seeing their friends and family. Birthdays and holiday gatherings were cancelled. For parents whose children were no longer able to attend school and who couldn't get childcare, the pressures of working from home while helping children with their studies were difficult to manage. For children who were no longer able to see their friends at school, or even meet them outside to play, life became very boring. For elderly or vulnerable people in hospitals and care homes who were no longer allowed to see visitors, the days seemed very long. Soon, many people began to feel lonely and depressed. William and Catherine wanted to do what they could to help and teamed up with an organization called Public Health England on a campaign called Every Mind Matters.

"THE LAST FEW WEEKS HAVE BEEN ANXIOUS AND UNSETTLING FOR EVERYONE. WE HAVE TO TAKE TIME TO SUPPORT EACH OTHER AND FIND WAYS TO LOOK AFTER OUR MENTAL HEALTH. IT IS GREAT TO SEE THE

MENTAL HEALTH SECTOR WORKING TOGETHER WITH THE NHS TO HELP PEOPLE KEEP ON TOP OF THEIR MENTAL WELL-BEING. BY PULLING TOGETHER AND TAKING SIMPLE STEPS EACH DAY, WE CAN ALL BE BETTER PREPARED FOR THE TIMES AHEAD."

The Duke and Duchess of Cambridge

To make sure people knew about the campaign, Catherine and William appeared on television to discuss how COVID-19 was affecting people's mental health and what they could do to protect themselves. They took part in a video in which they encouraged people to "make a plan" to protect their mental health and the mental health of those around them, and to seek help when things became too difficult.

A Murder in Minneapolis

In summer 2020, people all over the world took to the streets to protest about the murder of an unarmed black man named George Floyd in Minneapolis, USA. George Floyd was murdered by a police officer named Derek Chauvin while he was being arrested. The murder was caught on the phone of a teenager named Darnella Frazier, who posted the footage online. People were outraged by what they saw and took to the streets in protest. The unrest began in Minneapolis and spread to other cities in the USA.

People saw the murder of George Floyd, the

latest in a long line of racist killings, as proof that black people were treated as if their lives didn't matter as much as those of white people.

The protests in Minneapolis inspired racial justice demonstrations around the world. Some of the largest protests outside of the USA took place in cities around the United Kingdom, where campaigners wanted to draw attention to racism in British institutions such as the police force. The protests were organized by a movement named Black Lives Matter.

BLACK LIVES MATTER

Black Lives Matter is a non-profit organization that works to highlight and put an end to the injustice and violence experienced by Black people around the world. Black Lives Matter began in 2013 following the shooting of a Black American teenager named Trayvon Martin by a white man named George Zimmerman in February 2012. Zimmerman saw Trayvon walking in his neighbourhood and thought he looked suspicious. He called the police, who advised him not to approach the seventeen-year-old. Instead Zimmerman followed Trayvon, argued with him and shot him dead. At first, George Zimmerman was not charged, but after massive protests he was arrested and charged with murder. When Zimmerman appeared in court he claimed that despite Trayvon being unarmed, he had killed him in self-defence. The court believed him and Zimmerman was found not guilty. This made many people very angry as they believed it showed how the police and court system treated Black people as if their lives did not matter. When people posted about the case on social media they used the hashtag #BlackLivesMatter.

From here, Black Lives Matter grew into an organization operating in the USA, the United Kingdom and Canada.

As part of the protests, and to highlight how racism was part of everyday life in the United Kingdom, protestors graffitied and tore down statues of historical figures such as slave traders and politicians.

In Bristol, in the southwest of England, protestors tore down a statue of a man named Edward Colston and threw it into the sea. Edward Colston lived in Bristol during the 1600s and was deputy governor of a business called the Royal African Company.

THE ROYAL AFRICAN COMPANY

The Royal African Company was set up in 1672 by King Charles II and his brother the Duke of York (later King James II). It was granted exclusive rights to the trade and transportation of enslaved African people. Between 1672 and 1731, more than 180,000 enslaved men, women and children were taken from West Africa on ships operated by the Royal African Company and sold to the owners of plantations in the Caribbean and North America. By 1700, the Royal African Company was the world's largest trader in slaves. Conditions on these ships were deadly. To maximize profits, people were shackled together to cram as many as possible onboard. Disease and brutal treatment were common and as many as two out of every ten people died on the journey.

Edward Colston made a great deal of money working for the Royal African Company, trading in enslaved African people. When he died in 1721, he left a lot of money to charity. This money was used to fund initiatives around the city of Bristol, such as public buildings and scholarships. Because of the wealth he brought to the city, many places around Bristol were named after Colston, and a statue was erected in his honour, but while he brought wealth to some of the white people living in Bristol, he had caused the deaths of tens of thousands of Black people and misery for countless more and for their descendants.

As protestors took to the streets, others showed their support on social media platforms such as Twitter, TikTok and Facebook. Concerned by how the killing of George Floyd affected people's mental health, William and Catherine showed their support on Instagram through their mental health initiative, Heads Together (see page 214).

"HEADS TOGETHER STANDS WITH THE BLACK COMMUNITY. TODAY AND EVERY DAY. THIS IS A

REMINDER TO ALL THAT YOUR MENTAL HEALTH MATTERS, AND OUR CHARITY PARTNERS ARE THERE FOR YOU IF YOU NEED SUPPORT. BLACK LIVES MATTER. TODAY AND EVERY DAY."

Heads Together Instagram post

The Cambridges Say Thank You

In December 2020, William and Catherine donned their masks to embark on a three-day tour of the United Kingdom on board the royal train.

The tour was to thank frontline staff in hospitals and clinics around the country. The Cambridges travelled more than 1,250 miles around England, Scotland and Wales to meet with people who had gone above and beyond in response to the COVID-19 pandemic. William and Catherine met hospital workers, teachers and care workers to find out how they were being affected by the pandemic and to thank them for their hard work serving their communities.

Many people were glad to see the couple, though others criticized them for travelling around the country and meeting people when others were not allowed to see their own families.

Christmas Is Cancelled

For a lot of people, being separated from their families was very hard. People hoped that they would be able to get together over the Christmas holidays, when the government planned to relax the rules. Sadly this was not to be for many. Just days before Christmas, Prime Minister Boris Johnson announced that COVID-19 was more contagious than ever and that people living in areas where there had been a lot of cases could no longer mix with people they did not already live with.

While many families were kept apart by this second lockdown, this was not the only reason William didn't spend Christmas with his brother and his family in 2020. In fact, even though there were no restrictions on phone calls, William and his brother rarely spoke.

An Interview with the Sussexes

In March 2021, Harry and Meghan, now the Duke and Duchess of Sussex, agreed to take part in an interview with a US talk show host named Oprah Winfrey. During this interview, Harry and Meghan claimed that Charles no longer accepted Harry's calls and that he and William had barely spoken to one another since he left the UK. Meghan and Harry revealed how unhappy they had been and how they felt they weren't supported by the royal family. Meghan claimed that she had been treated unfairly by the press, and explained how some of the racist stories that were printed affected her mental health. They also claimed that some of the racism Meghan experienced came from within the royal family itself.

Following the interview, the Palace issued a statement claiming that the royal family were "saddened" to discover how unhappy Harry and Meghan had been.

"THE ISSUES RAISED, PARTICULARLY THAT OF RACE, ARE CONCERNING. WHILST SOME RECOLLECTIONS MAY

VARY, THEY ARE TAKEN VERY SERIOUSLY AND WILL BE ADDRESSED BY THE FAMILY PRIVATELY. HARRY, MEGHAN AND ARCHIE WILL ALWAYS BE MUCH-LOVED FAMILY MEMBERS."

Buckingham Palace

Shortly after the interview aired, William – who rarely commented on stories in the press – felt compelled to respond, after a visit to a school in East London, when asked whether his family was racist.

"WE ARE VERY MUCH NOT A RACIST FAMILY."

William, Prince of Wales

Carrying On

William made no further comment about the interview, or about his relationship with his brother and Meghan. For William, these matters were private. He remembered how embarrassed he had been when both his mother and his father had given interviews while he was growing up, and he wasn't about to do the same.

Instead, William wanted to carry on with his work, and his duty to his family.

With Harry and Meghan leaving, William and Catherine picked up much of the work they had been doing. The Cambridges were busier than ever. Also, William's grandmother was unable to perform her public duties, because she and Prince Philip had been advised to shield themselves from the risk of exposure to COVID-19, due to their age.

An Extraordinary Man

On 9 April 2021, William's grandfather Prince Philip, Duke of Edinburgh, passed away at Windsor Castle. His funeral took place at St George's Chapel, Windsor, on 17 April 2021. Unlike other royal funerals, which attracted crowds of people to pay their respects, COVID-19 restrictions meant that Prince Philip's was attended by just thirty members of his family and close friends, who sat separately and wore masks.

William was very sad to lose his grandfather but was grateful for all the time they had spent together and the memories his own children were able to make with him.

"MY GRANDFATHER WAS AN EXTRAORDINARY

MAN AND PART OF AN EXTRAORDINARY GENERATION. CATHERINE AND I WILL CONTINUE TO DO WHAT HE WOULD HAVE WANTED AND WILL SUPPORT THE QUEEN IN THE YEARS AHEAD. I WILL MISS MY GRANDPA, BUT I KNOW HE WOULD WANT US TO GET ON WITH THE JOB."

William, Prince of Wales

Honouring a Legacy

One of the ways William paid tribute to his grandfather was in his work for the environment. Prince Philip loved the natural world and had always been particularly interested in charities that worked to protect it.

"THE CONSERVATION OF NATURE, THE PROPER CARE FOR THE HUMAN ENVIRONMENT AND A GENERAL CONCERN FOR THE LONG-TERM FUTURE OF THE WHOLE OF OUR

PLANET ARE ABSOLUTELY VITAL IF FUTURE GENERATIONS ARE TO HAVE A CHANCE TO ENJOY THEIR EXISTENCE ON THIS EARTH."

Prince Philip, Duke of Edinburgh, 1970

William was inspired by his grandfather's work and hoped to pass on a love of the environment to his own children. But while William was glad to carry on Philip's efforts, he said it would be a disaster if George was having to speak about the same problems thirty years from now. He felt it was time to be ambitious and come up with a solution once and for all.

The Earthshot Prize

In 2019, William announced the launch of the Earthshot Prize. The name was inspired by President John F. Kennedy, who in 1961 proposed to the US Congress that the United States should work towards landing people on the moon by the end of that decade.

"WE CHOOSE TO GO TO THE MOON IN THIS DECADE AND DO THE OTHER THINGS, NOT BECAUSE THEY ARE EASY, BUT BECAUSE THEY ARE HARD, BECAUSE

THAT GOAL WILL SERVE TO ORGANIZE AND MEASURE THE BEST OF OUR ENERGIES AND SKILLS, BECAUSE THAT CHALLENGE IS ONE THAT WE ARE WILLING TO ACCEPT, ONE WE ARE UNWILLING TO POSTPONE, AND ONE WHICH WE INTEND TO WIN."

President John F. Kennedy

President Kennedy's ambitious "moon shot" excited people. It inspired them to work together to come up with solutions and new technology more quickly than they ever had before, so a human could set foot on the moon. On 21 July 1969, US astronaut Neil Armstrong became the first person to do just that.

Celebrating Solutions

William wanted Earthshot to inspire people to work towards solving the planet's biggest problems. He wanted to change the conversation on the environment from one about the damage that had been done, to one celebrating the work that was going on to preserve and protect it.

The Earthshot Prize makes awards of £1 million to the winning environmental projects in five categories:

- Protect and restore nature
- Clean our air
- Revive our oceans
- Build a waste-free world
- Fix our climate.

The first award ceremony took place in 2021 at Alexandra Palace in London and the winners included a coral farming project based in the Bahamas and a government scheme in the Republic of Costa Rica that rewards local people for their work preserving and restoring their local environment. The awards were presented by celebrities such as Emma Thompson and David Oyelowo and featured performances by Coldplay, Ed Sheeran and KSI. William was delighted by the event and by the fact it was a celebration of the work that was being done to protect the environment. William wanted Earthshot to become the biggest and most talked about environmental prize in history, so he hoped the next awards would be even bigger and better.

A Focus on the Early Years

While William had been working on Earthshot, Catherine had been busy with her work focusing on early-years education. In 2019, she began to research how people's early life affected their learning, and used what she discovered to launch a new project. In 2021, Kensington Palace announced that Catherine was opening a centre dedicated to the role early childhood played in the rest of people's lives.

"THE EARLY YEARS ARE NOT SIMPLY ABOUT HOW WE RAISE OUR CHILDREN. THEY ARE ABOUT THE SOCIETY WE WILL BECOME."

Catherine, Duchess of Cambridge

The Royal Foundation Centre for Early Childhood would bring scientists together with people who worked in early-years education to conduct new research. The aim was to discover new methods of improving children's early-years experiences.

William's work with the Earthshot Prize and Catherine's with the Royal Foundation Centre for Early Childhood tackle very different issues, but they both focus on building a better future. William and Catherine want to use their influence to help create a better world for everyone, including the royal family.

A ROYAL RECKONING

The year 2022 was a big year for the royal family as it was the year that Queen Elizabeth II celebrated her Platinum Jubilee, marking seventy years since she ascended the throne. To mark the occasion, the Palace planned a series of events culminating with a special celebration weekend in June. The events included national and international tours, visits, galas, garden parties, dinners, concerts and parades, as well as hundreds of local street parties.

The Jubilee was a celebration, but it was also tinged with sadness, because as people gathered it soon became obvious that somebody very important was often missing – the queen herself. Due to concerns for her health, Elizabeth was advised by palace doctors to rest. To make sure the celebrations went without a hitch, William and Catherine were more than happy to do their part, but even as the fun began, there was a sense that the reign of Elizabeth II was coming to an end.

Royals on Tour

As part of the Jubilee celebrations, the Palace had scheduled royal tours of the United Kingdom and other countries. As the queen was not able to travel herself, her family stepped in.

In March 2022, William and Catherine visited Belize, Jamaica and the Bahamas as part of the Platinum Jubilee tour. The purpose of the visit was to strengthen ties with members of the Commonwealth. But the tour did not go to plan – in fact, it was a disaster. The cheering crowds that had greeted Queen Elizabeth in the early years of her reign were nowhere to be seen, and in their place stood protestors.

In Belize, local people protested their arrival and events had to be cancelled. In Jamaica, protestors in Kingston called for William to apologize for slavery and pay reparations for the unpaid work of their ancestors, while the Jamaican government announced that they planned to become a republic, removing the queen as their head of state. While in Jamaica, William spoke about the legacy of slavery.

"I WANT TO EXPRESS MY PROFOUND SORROW. SLAVERY WAS ABHORRENT, AND IT SHOULD NEVER HAVE HAPPENED."

William, Duke of Cambridge

But many didn't feel he had gone far enough. In the Bahamas, a government committee signed a letter asking William to apologize for slavery and for reparations to be paid.

While for some people, the royal family are a source of pride and a symbol of the rich history of the United Kingdom, for many others around the world, royalty represents a painful legacy of enslavement and colonialism (see page 233).

It was clear from William and Catherine's visit that people's opinion of the monarchy in 2022 was very different from the opinions of their parents and grandparents when Queen Elizabeth came to the throne seventy years before. People had changed and they wanted that change to be acknowledged. The monarchy would have to change too if it was going to survive.

Closer to home, there were other upheavals.

The War in Ukraine

On 22 February 2022, Russian president Vladimir Putin ordered his troops, stationed on the Ukrainian border, to launch an attack on

Ukraine. President Putin did this because he did not want Ukraine to form alliances with countries he saw as a threat to Russia.

From 1922 to 1991, Russia and Ukraine, as well as countries such as Belarus, were part of a union of countries called the Soviet Union or USSR. After the Soviet Union split in 1991, these countries became independent. They started forming their own governments and relationships with other countries around the world. President Putin didn't want countries like Ukraine joining an alliance called the North Atlantic Treaty Organization (NATO). NATO is made up of countries in North America and Europe whose leaders signed an agreement to protect one another should they be attacked.

HOW THIS AFFECTED THE UNITED KINGDOM

Although Ukraine was not yet a member of NATO, after the country was attacked, other nations offered their support by sending arms to help the Ukrainian forces fight the Russians. They also pledged aid and implemented sanctions against Russia. Sanctions are a kind of political punishment designed to hurt the economy of a country they are imposed on. These sanctions included banning the import of Russian goods. In response, Vladimir Putin ordered the Russian gas industry to stop supplying as much gas to Europe. Gas is used to fuel power stations to produce electricity and to heat people's homes. Before the war in Ukraine, Russia supplied 40 per cent of the gas used in Europe. Cutting the supply caused the price of gas in Europe and the United Kingdom to increase, and people's bills to rise.

Official Business

As well as going on tours on behalf of the queen, William was also asked to help his father fulfil some of his grandmother's other obligations. On 10 May 2022, William accompanied his father to Westminster as he delivered a speech at the State Opening of Parliament.

Charles delivered the speech on behalf of his mother, but as he was not the monarch he could not wear the State Crown or the Robes of State. Instead, to represent the queen's presence, the State Crown was carried on a velvet pillow and placed on a table at Charles's side.

Parliament had a lot to do, as life in the United Kingdom was becoming very difficult for a lot of people.

THE COST OF LIVING CRISIS

The prices of the things for sale in shops go up all the time. This is called inflation. Inflation measures how much more something costs this year compared to how much it was the year before. While prices go up most years, in the year 2022, almost everything in the United Kingdom was much more expensive than it had been the year before, due to a high rate of inflation. While inflation made everything more expensive, people's income did not rise by much. It became more difficult for people to afford the things they were able to buy the year before. People were already finding it hard to pay their living expenses – the cost of things like food, energy (gas and electricity), taxes, transportation and accommodation.

One of the roles of the monarch is to convey honours on people at a ceremony called an investiture. As well as attending the opening of parliament, William was also asked to perform investitures on his grandmother's behalf. An honour is an award recognizing the good work people have done. In the United Kingdom, a list of people who are receiving honours is published twice a year.

A Family on the Move

In August 2022, William and Catherine announced that they would soon be moving their family to Adelaide Cottage, a four-bedroomed house close to Windsor Castle. Moving to Windsor would allow William to be closer to his grandmother, who not only relied on his help in performing her duties, but also for his advice on the future of the monarchy, a future that was coming closer every day.

A Final Journey

On 8 September 2022, William received a call informing him that the queen had fallen very ill at Balmoral, and that he should travel there as quickly as he could. William headed immediately for the airport, where he boarded a plane to Aberdeen.

Balmoral was a special place for William – he had many happy memories of times spent there with his grandparents and it was where they supported him when he found out his mother had died.

Sadly, William didn't make it in time. Queen Elizabeth II died at 3.10 p.m. with her son, Charles, and her daughter, Anne, by her side. After her death, William walked outside and saw five rainbows above the castle.

"I THANK HER FOR THE KINDNESS SHE SHOWED MY FAMILY AND ME. AND I THANK HER ON BEHALF OF MY GENERATION FOR PROVIDING AN EXAMPLE OF SERVICE AND DIGNITY IN PUBLIC LIFE THAT WAS FROM A DIFFERENT AGE, BUT ALWAYS

RELEVANT TO US ALL.
MY GRANDMOTHER
FAMOUSLY SAID THAT
GRIEF WAS THE PRICE
WE PAY FOR LOVE. ALL
OF THE SADNESS WE
WILL FEEL IN THE
COMING WEEKS WILL
BE TESTAMENT TO THE
LOVE WE FELT FOR OUR
EXTRAORDINARY QUEEN."

William, Prince of Wales

In the United Kingdom, when the monarch dies their heir automatically accedes to the throne and becomes king or queen. This meant William's father was now king. In fact, Charles's full title was "His Majesty Charles the Third, by the Grace of God, of the United Kingdom of Great Britain and Northern Ireland and of His other Realms and Territories King, Head of the Commonwealth, Defender of the Faith".

As king, Charles would have many more duties, and would no longer be able to spend time working with the charities he cared so much about.

As heir to the throne, William would now take on many of the titles that had belonged to his father. Instead of being the Duke and Duchess of Cambridge, William and Catherine would now become the Prince and Princess of Wales. As well as being given the title Prince of Wales, William would inherit the title Duke of Cornwall and with it the wealthy Duchy Estate (see page 163).

A Final Goodbye

Queen Elizabeth's funeral took place on 19 September 2022. As head of state, her funeral was a State Funeral, which meant it was a national occasion. Leaders from around the world flew in to pay their respects, including US president Joe Biden, New Zealand prime minister Jacinda Ardern, Canadian prime minister Justin Trudeau, Emperor Naruhito of Japan, King Letsie III of Lesotho and Barbadian president Sandra Mason.

The queen's funeral was a difficult day for William and Catherine, not only because they were saying goodbye to William's grandmother, but also because it meant spending time with Harry and Meghan.

Prince William walked in the funeral procession behind the coffin to Westminster Abbey, alongside his father King Charles III, his brother Prince Harry, his uncles Prince Andrew and Prince Edward, and his aunt Princess Anne.

Before the procession William and Harry joked that it was a familiar journey, because it was the same route they had walked together behind their mother's coffin when they were boys.

"AT LEAST WE KNOW THE WAY."

Harry, Duke of Sussex

William said in a conversation with Kate and Harry, filmed for Heads Together, that the death of their mother at such a young age had left the brothers "uniquely bonded" by what they had been through – but now that bond was in tatters.

A Broken Bond

The relationship between the two couples had been under strain since before Harry and Meghan married, but became much worse after the Sussexes announced they were stepping down from royal life (see page 223). When they left,

William and Catherine had to take on many of their charities and commitments but this wasn't all they had been left to deal with. After leaving the family, the Duke and Duchess of Sussex had given interviews to the press about their life in the royal family, and had made it clear they had more to say. William was angry with his brother for having spoken publicly about matters that he felt should be private. And he was wary of talking with his brother in case Harry decided to share his words with the press.

William was right to be wary. In December 2022, Harry and Meghan released a documentary series on Netflix about their life before leaving the royal family, in which they claimed that palace staff, prompted by members of the royal family, had deliberately given the press false stories about Meghan.

William did not respond directly to the interview, though palace sources claimed he was horrified and embarrassed. William might be a public figure, but he was a private person. Rather than comment on Harry's claims, William tried to focus on work.

Spare

In January 2023, Harry released an autobiography titled *Spare*. The title was taken from the phrase he had heard often growing up, when people referred to his father, Prince Charles, having an heir, William, and a spare, Harry, in case something happened to the elder son. Harry said that he wrote the book because he was tired of reading stories about himself in the press that weren't true. He wanted the chance to tell his own story. In his book, Harry wrote about growing up in the royal family and how he and William did not always get along. Harry claimed that his stepmother, Camilla, gave stories to the press about William and Harry when they were growing up.

According to Harry, William and Catherine disliked Meghan, and deliberately let the media believe that she was the cause of the rift within the family. Harry also claimed that William had pushed him over and had tried to provoke a fight.

The pictures Harry painted of royal family life were not flattering, and many people were angry with him and didn't think he should be invited to attend his father's coronation ceremony. Harry said he would only attend if he was given an apology for how he was treated.

Looking to the Future

William did not respond to Harry's accusations, though palace sources claimed that William was very angry and wasn't sure if he would be able to trust his brother again.

William wanted to focus on the future – on his father's coronation, his children and his new role as Prince of Wales.

The coronation of King Charles III was scheduled to take place on 6 May 2023, and promised to be a very different occasion to that of Elizabeth II. With many people struggling to pay their bills and feed their families, spending millions of pounds of public money on a ceremony was frowned upon. Charles wanted his coronation to keep some elements of tradition, but also reflect a more modern and less expensive monarchy. One of the ways Charles's coronation would be different was that there would be fewer guests. While Queen Elizabeth's coronation saw more than 8,000 people in specially built seats within the abbey, Charles planned to invite just 2,000. King Charles's ceremony would also be shorter. His mother's ceremony had taken nearly four hours, whereas Charles wanted his to be conducted in sixty minutes.

A Very Different Reign

As well as a different coronation, Charles's reign would not be like his mother's. Charles has a very different personality to Elizabeth – she was one of the most recognizable people on the planet, but very few people actually knew her or how she felt about things. As Prince of Wales, Charles had made his opinions known. That might not be appropriate for the king, but time would tell if he was able to keep his strong views to himself.

Charles's reign would be much shorter than his mother's. Whereas Elizabeth came to the throne when she was just 25 years old, the new king was 73. But this did mean that he had William and his wife Catherine there to support him, and in so doing they could prepare for their own future as king and queen.

Looking to the Future Together

When William and Catherine married, journalists wrote about how they had revived the monarchy. Both of them were keen to carry on doing just that – not only to secure their own position, but to lay a solid path for their son George.

On their travels, William and Catherine had seen first-hand how attitudes to the monarchy and the royal family had changed around the world, and they knew that to survive into the future, the royal family and the monarch would need to acknowledge the past.

In an interview, William said that in quiet moments he did sometimes think about the kind of king he would be.

"I THINK THE ROYAL FAMILY HAS TO MODERNIZE AND DEVELOP AS IT GOES ALONG AND IT HAS TO STAY RELEVANT, AND THE CHALLENGE FOR ME IS HOW DO I MAKE THE ROYAL FAMILY RELEVANT?"

William, Prince of Wales

William has known what his future held since he was a little boy – that one day, when his father dies, he will be king. He hopes that day is a long way off, but he knows that when the time comes, he and Catherine will tackle the challenge side by side.

ABOUT THE AUTHOR

Sally Morgan was born in Malaysia but grew up in England. She studied Literature and Classics at university. After graduating, she worked as a bookseller and as an editor before becoming a full-time writer. She is the author of many books including *Dream Big* and the *My Best Friend* series. Sally lives in Minneapolis, USA, with her husband and two children.

GLOSSARY

Actor – a person whose job it is to play a character in a film, television series or a play.

Catwalk – a narrow platform where models walk to display clothes in a fashion show.

Charity – an organization that raises money for and provides help to those in need.

Commonwealth of Nations – an international association which includes the United Kingdom and countries that used to be part of the British Empire. Other countries are also able to join.

Coronation – the ceremony crowning a monarch.

COVID-19 – a family of viruses that often affects animals, but sometimes moves from animals to humans. COVID-19 is a new virus that affects humans.

Government – a group of people that have the authority to rule a country.

Graduation – a ceremony for students to receive a degree or a diploma after successfully completing their studies.

Heir – a person that will legally inherit the property or rank of another person on that person's death.

Interview – a meeting between some people, usually formal, and for the purpose of answering questions.

Mental health – a person's condition related to their emotional and psychological well-being.

Monarchy – a type of government which recognizes a king or queen as head of state, even though they may not hold any political power.

National Curriculum – a set of subjects and guidelines used by primary and secondary schools.

NHS – National Health Service. The service began in 1948 to provide healthcare to everyone in the United Kingdom free at the point of use, but paid for by taxes.

Olympic Games – a multi-sports competition participated in by countries around the world, which originated in ancient Greece.

Pandemic – sudden and widespread outbreak of an infectious disease.

Paparazzi – independent photographers who follow people such as celebrities in order to get photographs of them to sell to the media.

Parliament – the part of government that has the power to make laws. Parliament also oversees the work of the government and represents the general public.

Patron – someone who provides support to a person, organization or cause.

Protest – a public action or statement that expresses disapproval for something.

Queen Consort – the wife of a currently reigning king.

Racism – the belief that different races possess different characteristics or qualities which make them inferior or superior to one another, often resulting in prejudice or discrimination.

Reign – the period of time a monarch rules.

Responsibility – a duty to do something that is required or expected of you.

Training – the act of teaching someone or something a set of skills, behaviours or techniques.

University – a high-level place of education where students go to study for a degree or do academic research.

Walkabout – when members of the royal family take some time during their visit to personally meet people who have come to see them.

War – a state of armed conflict between two or more countries or groups of people.

INDEX

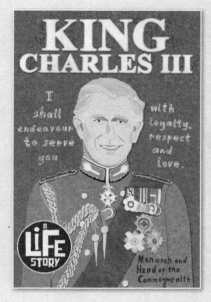

KATHERINE JOHNSON

There will always be SCIENCE, ENGINEERING and TECHNOLOGY.

And there will always always be MATHEMATICS.

A LiFE STORY

NASA Mathematician

STEPHEN HAWKING

Without IMPERFECTION neither YOU nor I would EXIST.

A LiFE STORY

Theoretical Physicist

ALAN TURING

I propose to consider the question, 'Can machines think?'

A LiFE STORY

Computer Scientist

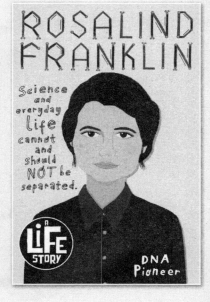

ROSALIND FRANKLIN

Science and everyday life cannot and should NOT be separated.

A LiFE STORY

DNA Pioneer

SERENA WILLIAMS

WHATEVER fear I have INSIDE me, my DESIRE to WIN is always STRONGER.

A LiFE STORY

Tennis Player

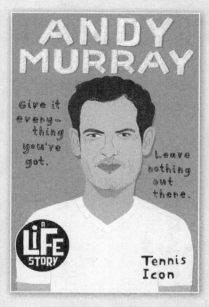

ANDY MURRAY

Give it everything you've got.

Leave nothing out there.

A LiFE STORY

Tennis Icon

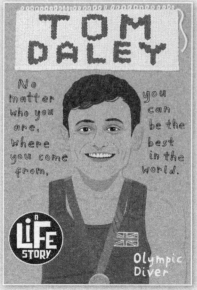

TOM DALEY

No matter who you are, where you come from, you can be the best in the world.

A LiFE STORY

Olympic Diver

EMMA RADUCANU

Playing sport, and having to be bold on the court and fearless and fight, its given me inner strength.

A LiFE STORY

Tennis Superstar